PARENTING & FAMILIES

# WHOLEHEARTED LEARNING: A Guidebook for Parents

Rediscovering God's Loving Instructions

RON K. LUNDQUIST, M.ED.
M.A. IN BIBLICAL STUDIES

Biblically-based family flourishing is what this marvelous book, *Wholehearted Learning*, is all about. Based on his own life experiences founded in clearly explained biblical truths, Ron Lundquist describes and then narrates how experiential heart-to-heart relational living proves itself true!

*William F. Cox, Jr., PhD, former Dean,*
*School of Education, Regent University*

Many child-rearing books apply a toxic level of institutional bias through socio-political theories and abstract concepts. Ron Lundquist addresses the *real* issues of how a parent—with a job, a life, a family to feed, and boots on the ground instead of a castle in the air—should train up a child in the way he or she should go. Put the psychology books and social propaganda manuals back on the shelf, folks—*Wholehearted Learning* is a child-rearing book for real parents raising real children in the real world.

*Bill Bullock, AAL, Bullock Law Firm.*
*Also known as 'the Rabbi's son'*

Ron Lundquist not only reveals his heart for raising and nurturing the generations in his book *Wholehearted Learning*, but ultimately the Father's heart itself. Ron has sought the Lord, searched the scriptures, whittled and chiseled, to bring forth a deeper insight into the transformation process to "train up a child."

*Deborah Franz,*
*Ascension Ministries Int'l*

Ron Lundquist takes a deep Spirit-led dive into Scripture that systematically reveals God's wholehearted learning process. With his rich understanding of Hebrew, Ron shows the Father's loving heart and plan for His children as one harmonious expression throughout the Old and New Testaments. Every parent, pastor, and family counselor should have this invaluable resource on their bookshelf. I plan to have it on mine.

*Norman Franz, Senior Pastor,*
*Ascension Ministries, Int'l*

Xulon Press
2301 Lucien Way #415
Maitland, FL 32751
407.339.4217
www.xulonpress.com

***WHOLEHEARTED LEARNING:*** *A Guidebook for Parents*


Printed in the United States of America.

Paperback ISBN-13: 978-1-6628-1228-6
eBook ISBN-13: 978-1-6628-1229-3

# WHOLEHEARTED LEARNING:

## A Guidebook for Parents

Ron K. Lundquist, M.ED.
M.A. in Biblical Studies

XULON PRESS

# Table of Contents


Acknowledgments . . . . . . . . . . . . . . . . . . . . . . . . . . . . ix
Dedication . . . . . . . . . . . . . . . . . . . . . . . . . . . . . . . . xi
Introduction . . . . . . . . . . . . . . . . . . . . . . . . . . . . . . . xiii
How to Use This Guide . . . . . . . . . . . . . . . . . . . . . . . . . xxi

**Part 1: A Transformation of Thinking**

Chapter 1 Wholehearted Learning . . . . . . . . . . . . . . . . . . . 1
Chapter 2 Rediscovering a Radically New and Refreshing Way of Thinking and Living . . . . . . 11
Chapter 3 Wisdom Cries Out . . . . . . . . . . . . . . . . . . . . . . 21

**Part 2: Parents First**

Chapter 4 Parents First — The Starting Point . . . . . . . . . . 35
Chapter 5 Pathways of Life — God's Loving Instructions . . . . . . . . . . . . . . . . . 47
Chapter 6 Yahweh's Ten Loving Instructions — Loving God – His First Three Words . . . . . . . . 53
Chapter 7 Yahweh's Ten Loving Instructions — Loving God – His Fourth Word . . . . . . . . . . . . 69
Chapter 8 Yahweh's Ten Loving Instructions — Loving Your Neighbor–His Words Five to Ten . . . . . . . . . . . . . . . . . . . . . . . . . . . . . 81

## Part 3: Foundations Unlocked -at Home


Chapter 9 At Home — Putting It All Together. . . . . . . . 105
Chapter 10 Love and Bonding —
Relational Foundations . . . . . . . . . . . . . . . . . . . . 111
Chapter 11 Discipline — Relational Foundations . . . . . . . 133
Chapter 12 The Three Phases of Discipline —
Relational Foundations . . . . . . . . . . . . . . . . . . . . 149

Accepting the Challenge . . . . . . . . . . . . . . . . . . . . . . . . . . 173
Saplings of the LORD . . . . . . . . . . . . . . . . . . . . . . . . . . . 185
Bibliography . . . . . . . . . . . . . . . . . . . . . . . . . . . . . . . . . 189
Further Reading . . . . . . . . . . . . . . . . . . . . . . . . . . . . . . 193

# Acknowledgments

*Gifts...* from the storehouse of God's grace. The first, my beautiful and precious wife, Gretchen. Little did she (or we) know the journeys or adventures that were hidden deep beneath her marriage vows spoken to me, "Your God shall be my God, and where you go I will go"! From wilderness living to graduate school, she has been by my side. And as our three children were birthed while we traveled new and unexplored pathways, her sacrificial giving and caring for us all demonstrated unflinching consistency to the principles I write about in this book. She also stood by me through the inner healing process I needed in my own life. Thank you, my dear one!

As our lives were being changed and we began to discover the foundations for wholehearted learning, our three children became a part of our journey as we shed ideas and beliefs with which we had grown up while embracing new ones. Our family established newfound life together. Andrew (adventurer), Elizabeth (sparkly), and Jonathan (buddy) all hung in there as we continually searched for the pathways for learning, and living that leads to wholeness until the day each of them left our nest. As we played, laughed, and worked together, we learned many valuable lessons in the midst of the normal struggles of life. Much of this training now has become a part of their families as well. Andrew, Jonathan, and Elizabeth, you remain our most loved and cherished gifts! We are exceedingly grateful and proud for each one of you as you have blazed your unique paths after leaving home! Oh yes, I must also mention the gift of twelve grandchildren that have been added to our treasure chest as well!

Of course, I wouldn't be writing this without the gift of my parents. As I grew up in Colorado with two older brothers, our dad and mom demonstrated their constant and sacrificial love for us. That was quite an accomplishment, considering how mischievous the "three musketeers" were behind the scenes. There are untold stories of which they never knew. After I left home, their enduring love was often challenged by many changes and unexpected adventures in my journey of life with Gretchen and our children.

I also wish to thank William F. Cox Jr., PhD, Professor, School of Education, Regent University. Dr. Cox and I became close friends as I worked to complete a joint master's degree in education and biblical studies. We often talked of our shared vision of families being the foundation stone for all of life. His prayers and faithful encouragement never faltered. Thank you, my friend!

At just the right moment in my writing process, another gift was given to me. With great tenacity and skill, my editor, Kathy Groom, joined me in this journey with her insight and suggestions to help bring this project to completion. It's been a joy to have walked these steps together. Thank you, Kathy!

Finally, and how appropriate, I give my last kudos to our daughter, Elizabeth, who added her amazing talent as the cover and graphic designer for this book. Thanks, Sparkly!

# Dedication

To parents everywhere who desire to unlock this profound secret for themselves.

*The foundation for imparting wholehearted learning to your children begins by becoming role models for them—Lighthouses, in your homes, lighting the pathways for your children to follow.*

# Introduction

*I believe* the vocation of being a parent is perhaps the highest calling in this life. Unfortunately, most newlyweds and parents are inadequately prepared to fulfill this profound vocation with wisdom and understanding. To make matters worse, our world, our educational system, our trusted family values, all seem to be crumbling around us.

Early in our marriage, my wife Gretchen and I lived in extreme northern Wisconsin among rolling hardwood-covered hills, lakes, and fertile farmlands just a few miles south of Lake Superior. Living alone with scarce income, no electricity or running water, we were tested to the core. At night, beneath brilliant starlit skies, I hurled my cries from my heart to the heavens. I had such a deep desire within me to see the coming of the kingdom of God.

Then something good started happening in our lives and our home. We learned that our heavenly Father cares for, hears, and answers the requests of His children, and He loves entire households as well as every individual. God was answering those heart cries as we were learning how to walk with Him, applying His kingdom principles in our lives and in raising our children. It was as if our obedience to what God was showing us became a birthing process. We found that we were walking in pathways of life, not educational theory, resulting in both practical and fruitful outcomes. Our relationship with our heavenly Father brought our entire family into great joy, satisfaction, purpose, fulfillment, and enjoyment of one another—as well as remarkable accomplishments.

My goal in writing this guidebook is to provide a navigational GPS for parents who desire to lead their children into what I have chosen to call "wholehearted learning." I want to help open the door for others who have become confused by the array of educational theories and approaches being advocated today back to the foundations of wholehearted learning. My sole desire is to help guide parents in a direction that is biblically sound and practical.

There are principles within the treasure store of God's word that provide the foundations for wholehearted learning. One of these foundations is intimate and authentic relationships in the home. Ironically, as these foundations for wholehearted learning became established in our family, the most important things we were doing for the educational equipping of our children had little to do with formal education.

From my own experience and involvement in various formal educational settings with our children, as well as observations and discussions with educators in both public and Christian schools, the paramount issues that have emerged are *discipline* and *lack of motivation*—not academic accomplishment in the classroom. Note carefully, discipline and motivation are *character*, not academic, issues. Subpar academic performance may only be a symptom of an underlying cause. Often, foundational issues of poor academic achievement are either not understood or ignored. Pride and humanism have blocked the way to an authentic starting point of fixing our country's academic demise.

The development of character *and* academic achievement must both be present in the lives of students as measurements of success. Parents who do not grasp their strategic roles for establishing their own children's character at home will be unable to work in concert with instructors in more formal educational settings, attempting to fulfill their educational objectives.

In an amoral society and culture dangerously adrift, filled with family breakdowns and wounded relationships, there remains an active, loving God who cares and has revealed a plan for our children that works. He tenderly holds out this plan for a lost generation to rediscover. God reveals His plan to parents who pursue wholehearted learning for their children—a pathway of blessing, quality of life, and godly character, out of which flows academic achievement.

Usually, when thinking of education, the primary focus immediately centers on children. Educators and parents alike wrongly believe that learning begins with children in a formal classroom, often starting with pre-kindergarten. The approach to education in our culture, which focuses primarily on children while excluding parents, is upside down and failing on many fronts.

Wholehearted learning begins with parents, not children. And this learning starts at home, not in the classroom. Formal education can wait. Wholehearted learning begins outside the classroom—it originates in the home.

And it must start with the parents.

What in heaven's name do the personal lives of parents have to do with educating their children? Everything! Why? Because children have sensors that function on high alert as their perceptions develop about their world. Children's keen receptors quickly gain an understanding of the world around them from all their experiences in early childhood. All these experiences form a worldview in their hearts and minds. Children take in *who their parents are,* not just what they say. As children grow, they trivialize their parents' words but ingest what they *see* in the lives of their parents. Because parents' behavior and lifestyles are paramount to leading children into wholehearted learning, the first goal for us as parents must be to build personal lifestyles that will nurture our children's hearts and influence their minds.

Having dug deeply into Scripture has led me to these two truths that are inextricably connected: The "lifestyle" revealed in Scripture for parents leads to "wholehearted" learning for their children. In this book, I will share with you the rediscovery of bedrock for living and parenting. These eternal paths will provide enduring foundations in your lives and the lives of your children.

Gretchen and I thank God for leading us down these paths of Scriptural truth. They provided the most fertile soil for our children to develop and grow to their fullest potential. As our children grew, foundations were being modeled and planted in their lives. These foundations have become of immense worth for all subsequent formal and informal learning experiences.

Our only boast is that *God's ways work.*

Our oldest son Andrew graduated from the United States Air Force Academy. During the initial application process, he received three nominations from Virginia Congressman and Senators, where we were living at that time. Senator John Warner submitted his official nomination for Andrew's appointment to the USAF Academy. During high school, Andrew was an all-tournament basketball player, an excellent artist, and enjoyed drama and music as well. He has pioneered the founding of a computer web and software development company in partnership with others.

Our daughter Elizabeth began her significant courses of study ahead of the standard timeline. She is a talented writer with a degree in Journalism, using her skills to create businesses, and is a real estate agent. *Who's Who Among American High School Students* listed both Andrew and Elizabeth three times during consecutive high school years. Both were Valedictorians of their class, members of the National Honor Society, and elected to many student leadership positions throughout their high school years.

Our second son, Jonathan, apparently not to be outdone by his older brother and sister, skipped a grade, moving from the eighth grade into high school where he quickly moved to the top of his class. Subsequently, he, too, was nominated by *Who's Who Among American High School Students* and was the Valedictorian of his class. He is now working in the computer field as a program and software developer. All three now have families of their own.

While our children were growing up, we chose not to place undue stress on their grades or extracurricular school involvement. At times as they progressed and excelled, we would take them out to one of our favorite restaurants to enjoy a meal together in recognition of their excellent academic work and accomplishments, but we never offered any "pay off" for any of their achievements. Our goal instead was to provide a loving and secure home environment *where relationships mattered most.*

The priority, for Gretchen and me, was the development of our obedient relationship with God. Our second priority was loving and caring for each other as husband and wife. Our third priority was caring for our precious children. We attempted to keep our career choices secondary to those first relational priorities and aimed at providing the framework and resources to promote the best loving environment for all. For us, during the formative years of our children's lives, we made intentional occupational choices that allowed us the maximum time to develop and invest our lives into knowing God, loving each other, and being present with our children. Easy? By no means.

Rewarding? Absolutely!

We nurtured our children in an environment of love, intimacy, acceptance, discipline, encouragement, security, and peace. Their accomplishments have been their own.

They also experienced all the usual difficulties of life, frustrations, and failures that are a part of the human experience. That is why God has provided forgiveness and fresh starts for us all along the pathway of life.

To this day, our entire family continues to be the recipients of answers to that deep heart cry in the remote rolling hills of Wisconsin. The God of the Bible is real. He is a loving heavenly Father and has committed Himself to transform our lives if we allow it. In our relationship with Him, he desires for us to come into an intimate knowledge of who He is, who He truly is.

I have found there is often a vast difference between many of the religious world's commonly held views of who God is rather than who He truly is. During my ongoing journey, I have always been surprised by God's love, acceptance, and compassion for me. He is a God who is for us, not against us. Everything He has done through history—from the choosing of a nation to the giving of his Son to redeem all of humanity—reveals the loving and compassionate heart of a God who loves man and wants the very best for him. He is a loving Father whose deepest desire is to restore each person to wholeness.

In spiritual terms of our world today, we are living in a time of restoration. Like the sweet aroma of newly fallen rain, a fragrant breeze of God's Spirit is blowing throughout the earth, as the Creator of the universe draws His children back to Himself and His ways. God is restoring His eternal paths (Jeremiah 6:16). Effective and trustworthy foundations for living and raising children are being rediscovered by many. I am so grateful to have been carried along by a loving heavenly Father during this refreshing time of restoration. The transformation of our lives as parents has impacted the lives of our three children, and now, their children.

I chose to transcribe these principles so I could pass them along to our children as a guide for raising their children, and now for you as well, as you raise your own family.

May your discoveries in this guidebook result in personal transformation as you embrace the most fulfilling pathway for living and parenting. My prayer for you is that you will find invaluable treasures on God's pathway of life, freedom, and wisdom as you rediscover and learn how to raise wholehearted children.

# How to Use This Guide

**During** the great gold rush of the 1800s, gold prospectors painstakingly panned for gold in the ice-cold streams of the Rockies. With exceptional intensity, these explorers searched to find pure gold nuggets as they washed away the silt, exposing these treasures. Searching for priceless treasures in God's word requires a similar process.

Aspects of God's word that may initially appear to our unrenewed minds to be dust-laden rocks, later become invaluable treasures when they are revealed anew by the brilliant light of God's Holy Spirit. For those who search for them, there is a great reward. There are rich discoveries of immense value for those who desire to know them. God's ways and truth are utterly useful and completely trustworthy. They work in human experience. Correctly understood and applied, the richness and rewards that God's ways bring to living are unsurpassed.

I invite you to pray and approach this Scripture-filled guidebook with an open mind and an open heart. Getting to know God and discovering His ways is like going on a treasure hunt!

### This guidebook consists of three sections.

**Part 1:** "A transformation of thinking" and **Part 2:** "Parents First" are written to equip parents to become *role models* for their children. This roadmap provides the building materials for achieving this goal.

**Part 3:** "Foundations Unlocked—At Home" was written as a practical guide for implementing *relational learning* between parents and children in the home.

Finally, "Accepting the Challenge" concludes with a call to action as well as brief writings from our three children. Each one personally shares from their firsthand experiences of growing up within this framework.

If you wish to delve immediately into the practical foundations for relational learning for establishing wholehearted learning at home with your children, you will find that in Part 3. Remember that your greatest effectiveness in producing wholehearted learning for your children begins by fully understanding and implementing what I have written in Parts 1 and 2. Understanding the Hebraic model of learning is foundational to wholehearted learning. The Hebraic model of learning focuses upon *doing*. This model is introduced in Part 1.

The footnotes throughout provide abundant additional resources that will shed more light on what I have written. I recommend you take the time to dig deeper into these notes for greater understanding.

I suggest as you read you allow this material to germinate in your thoughts and hearts for a season. Allow yourself time to discover the transformation that awaits you. Search diligently. Read with your heart. Take time to ingest what you may discover so you might experience a transformation in your heart and mind. Wholehearted learning by your children will be formed and sculptured by what they observe being modeled by you as the parent.

# Part 1

# A Transformation of Thinking

## Chapter 1

# Wholehearted Learning

*As* we welcome our children into our lives and homes, we are confronted with significant questions. How do we raise and educate our children? Naturally, we want the best for them!

What is the best approach to raising and educating our children? Is how we raise our children connected to their ability to learn? Where does the mind fit into this process? Are emotions important? And what about the inner being or heart of our dear children? And in this whole process, how do we raise and educate our children in such a way that prepares them to live in the world of our day?

As if these questions aren't enough, we are caught in a confusing cultural crossfire. Every day we encounter an array of skirmishes between contradictory theories and opinions on the battlefield of parenting and education. Where can we find a pathway that yields some answers to these probing questions?

In his book, *To Know as We Are Known*, Parker J. Palmer has aptly framed the dilemma and quest for wholehearted learning with the following words:

"Many of us live one-eyed lives. We rely largely on the eye of the mind to form our image of reality. But today, more and more of us are opening the other eye, the eye of the heart, looking for realities to which the mind's eye is blind. Either eye alone is not enough. We need 'whole sight,' a vision of the world in which mind and heart unite 'as my two eyes make one in sight.' Our seeing shapes our being. Only as we see the whole can we and our world be whole."

As parents, we face breathtaking challenges in raising and educating our children. Man's advanced knowledge in the frontiers of genetic engineering and our techno culture has ushered man to precipitous choices—with *highly developed minds* and *undeveloped hearts*. It is difficult to imagine a time in human history when "whole sight" has not been more needed to help guide the applications of this knowledge for the good of humanity.

Moral choices are the inevitable outcomes of many scientific discoveries. For example, editing the genomes of early human embryos, eggs, and sperm is now possible. If edited embryos are used to start a pregnancy, the changes affect every cell in the body of any resulting child, that child's offspring, their offspring, and so on. To edit the structure of cells that begin human life presents profound moral questions.

How are *heart* capacities made to grow and to flourish, which subsequently become the foundations for the applied judgments and values of the mind's accomplishments, so that such discoveries lead to the wellness of individuals from the inside out as well as society as a whole?

Palmer continues, "With the mind's eye, we see a world of fact and reason. It is a cold and mechanical place, but we have built our lives there because it seemed predictable and safe. Today, in the age of nuclear science, our mind-made world has been found flawed and dangerous, even lethal. So, we open the eye of the heart and see another sight: a world warmed and transformed by the power of love, a vision of a community beyond the mind's capacity to see. We cannot forsake our hearts, and yet we cannot abandon our minds. How shall we bring together these two lines of sight? How shall we use both eyes to create not a blurry double image but one world, in all its dimensions, healed and made whole?"[1] Parker describes the underlying principle of wholehearted learning—raising our children to see the world through both their mind's eye as well as their heart.

King Solomon, who led his society into the most advanced of his day in world history,[2] labored to achieve his unparalleled accomplishments with "whole sight." Solomon's counsel for all individuals and social rank within his administration was, "Above all else, guard your heart, for it affects everything you do."[3]

The Hebrew language is rich with meaning often lost when translated into our English language. Another translation of these words of Solomon is, "Above all else, guard your heart, for it is the wellspring of life."[4] And another translation says, "Keep your heart with all vigilance, and above all that your guard, for out of it flow the springs of life."[5] Significantly, the heart as a wellspring[6] is the source of life and provides an escape from death. It is no wonder that Solomon's priority (above all else) was to guard his heart.

---

1 Parker Palmer, *To Know as We Are Known: A Spirituality of Education* (San Francisco: Harper & Row, 1983), xi.

2 Please see Chapter 3, footnote 31.

3 Prov. 4:23.

4 Prov. 4:23, (NIV).

5 Prov. 4:23, (AMP).

6 James Gilbertson, *PC Study Bible for Windows* (WA: Biblesoft, November, 1998). Brown-Driver-Brigg's definition of the Hebrew word: *towtsa'ah* or *totsa'ah*-issues of life (wellspring).

From a physiological standpoint, the heart organ is the supreme life-sustaining organ of the human body. A man's life and health depend to a large extent on the condition of his heart. A person may suffer the loss of many other organs and live. But his body will never be sustained with the failure of his heart. The general heart condition as it pumps life-sustaining blood through the entire body is paramount to a man's state of health. Man cannot live without his heart.

This physiological picture beautifully illustrates the hidden, nevertheless *real,* function, and principle influence of the inner being (heart) on everything that man does (attitudes, decisions, and activities).[7] Today it would be a gross understatement to say

---

7 "Heart…the inner self that thinks, feels, and decides. In the Bible, the word heart has a much broader meaning than it does to the modern mind. The heart is that which is central to man. Nearly all the references to the heart in the Bible refer to some aspect of human personality. In the Bible, all emotions are experienced by the heart: love and hate (Ps. 105:25; 1 Pet. 1:22); joy and sorrow (Eccles. 2:10; John 16:6); peace and bitterness (Ezek. 27:31; Col. 3:15); courage and fear (Gen. 42:28; Amos 2:16). The thinking processes of man are said to be carried out by the heart. This intellectual activity corresponds to what would be called mind in English. Thus, the heart may think (Esth. 6:6), understand (Job 38:36), imagine (Jer. 9:14), remember (Deut. 4:9), be wise (Prov. 2:10), and speak to itself (Deut. 7:17). Decision-making is also carried out by the heart. Purpose (Acts 11:23), intention (Heb. 4:12),

we are all witnesses to private and public opinions, conclusions, and conduct that are morally corrupt. Social media—including movies, TV, and national news—has become a billboard for an array of twisted personal beliefs. Previously private thoughts are now broadcast for the world to see, regardless of the moral implications and perverted influence on our children.

The enormous magnitude of the mind's accomplishments in our time has radically outdistanced the heart's capacities to direct everyone's private pathway into overall health and wellness, let alone become corporate prescriptions for society and culture.

Ignoring the heart as the paramount core to education has resulted in confusion, brokenness, and death.[8] Many writers regard the heart as the seat of the conscience and the will. The heart is understood to be the center of all a man's activities. It represents his understanding as well as his emotional nature. *The heart*

---

and will (Eph. 6:60) are all activities of the heart. Finally, heart often means someone's true character or personality. Purity or evil (Jer. 3:17; Matt. 5:8), sincerity or hardness (Exod. 4:21; Col. 3:22); and maturity or rebelliousness (Ps. 101:2; Jer. 5:23)—all these describe the heart or true character of individuals. God knows the heart of each person (1 Sam. 16:7). Since a person speaks and acts from his heart, he is to guard it well (Prov. 4:23; Matt. 15:18-19). The most important duty of man is to love God with the whole heart (Matt. 22:37). With the heart, man believes in Christ and so experiences both love from God and the presence of Christ in his heart (Rom. 5:5; 10:9-10; Eph. 3:17)." Ibid., Definition from *Nelson's Illustrated Bible Dictionary*.

8 Without wholehearted education, the healing remedies for corruption, or the hidden cancer of the heart, are overlooked. Internal death (corruption is the central focus...not physical death) is a condition of being marred or disfigured within...the demoralization of heart and life through sin (Gen. 6:12; Deut. 9:12), resulting in those sinful habits and practices that defile and ruin men (Rom. 8:21; 2 Pet. 2:19). Isaiah describes this as the "pit of nothingness," i.e. of destruction. (Isa. 38:17). "Indeed, it was for my own peace that I had great bitterness; but You have lovingly delivered my soul from the pit of corruption, for You have cast all my sins behind Your back (NKJ). Notice clearly that Isaiah's joy is found in his being rescued *in this life*, not in the life to come.

*represents man's true self.* A man may be one thing outwardly and something else within.

Our western mindset and a purely academic approach to education have in part blinded us to the necessity and value for wholehearted education.[9] Solomon, who excelled in all learning and knowledge, drew from a deep wellspring which far surpassed, yet, obviously included all his mental faculties.

The word *brain*, as startling as it may seem, is not in the Old Testament. The *mind* occurs 39 times. There are over 700 references to the *heart!* King David and his son Solomon, were, and will always be remembered as, two of this world's most distinguished world leaders.[10] Both led their nation out of the wellspring of their hearts, something far deeper and more substantial than just their mental activities. The archival record of David, king and head of state, reads, "So he shepherded them *according to the integrity of his heart* and guided them by the discernment and skillfulness which *controlled* his hands." [italics mine][11]

With these thoughts as a background, consider once again what Solomon is saying in Proverbs 4:23. "*Keep* your heart with all vigilance, and *above all* that your guard, for out of it flow the springs of life." [italics mine] The word *keep* is a close synonym to the much more common Hebrew verb *Samar*, which means to keep or tend, in the sense of taking care of. God first gave Adam the divine instruction to tend and keep (*Samar*) the garden for his well-being.[12] Adam was to maintain, protect, preserve, and attend to the garden. Solomon is saying, priority number one for man, *before all else*, is to give careful attention to his own heart. Is this

---

9 The problem of Western thinking as a central obstacle to wholehearted education is addressed in Chapter 2.

10 See Chapter 3, footnote 31.

11 Ps. 78:72, (NAS, AMP).

12 Gen. 2:15.

the first activity captivating the hearts of men and women today, personally, educationally? The spread of the infectious cancer of corruption throughout our culture today is the outcome of a misplaced priority to guard and tend one's own heart.

As crucial as preservation and protection are, to keep or tend includes another vital aspect: *nurturing*. Such nurturing comes from listening to God's voice. Listening is much deeper than merely hearing the words themselves. The objective of most Western learning is to store facts in the learner's mind, just like a computer store byte in a computer memory chip. Most education does not have to pass beyond the mind gate—namely the cognitive or mental faculties of the learner—to enter the more extensive realms of the heart, as discussed previously. Generally, the intellectual achievements of the learner are tested and judged by the learner's ability to recall and process the data and subject matter already "taught." Hence, those who display the "best" one-eyed learning are most recognized, applauded, and rewarded with academic scholarships to pursue even more concentrated one-eyed educational goals. This mental prowess often is rewarded with the highest paying salaries. Unfortunately, these talents many times are undermined, squandered, or wasted because of the lack of "whole sight" in the application and use of such knowledge.

In contrast, *insight* and *discretion* grow out of *relational listening* to a loving God. Such insight and discretion are not unreasonable...but often beyond reason. In two-eyed learning, listening and subsequent learning are not mere mental activities. Wholehearted learning consists of three elements, all of which are related to heart issues.

- The first element of wholehearted learning is *to attend.* Learning of this nature first is accomplished with a keenness on the learner's part to listen while exercising proper discretion *to perceive a matter accurately.*[13]

- Secondly, having understood, the learner *agrees (consents)* with truth or the truthfully articulated voice of God, which is consistent with God's word.
- Thirdly, an inner agreement with God's truth results in *obedience* or *submission* to that which has been taught or heard.[14]

Personal wholeness, conduct, and life-giving action for others will always be the outcome of wholehearted learning. Listening, learning, and living are inextricably linked together.

---

[13] Man is created in God's image (Gen. 1:27). As an object of God's loving care, God has provided for all of man's needs in both the physical (Gen. 1:28-29) and spiritual realms (Matt. 4:4). In order to live in the reality of God's truth in both the physical and spiritual realms, man requires understanding that is greater than his own. Isaiah writes, "My thoughts are completely different from yours," says the LORD. "And my ways are far beyond anything you could imagine. For just as the heavens are higher than the earth, so are my ways higher than your ways and my thoughts higher than your thoughts." (Isa 55:8-9). In Proverbs 28:26, Solomon writes, "Trusting oneself is foolish, but those who walk in wisdom are safe." God desires that man has an accurate perception of all truth in the physical and spiritual worlds. Deuteronomy 29:29 says, "There are secrets the Lord your God has not revealed to us, but these words that he has revealed are for us and our children to obey forever." (TLB) In authentic biblical learning, *wisdom*, which is the canon of eternally true principles that explain reality and govern morality is the primary goal of learning. All other learned and acquired knowledge is built upon this foundation.

[14] The *nature* of biblical learning is uniquely different than any other approach to learning. Authentic biblical learning forms an inward *relationship* of the learner with *the Truth*. There is a two-way movement of *persons* searching for each other (see Chapters 2-3). As Parker Palmer writes in his book, *To Know as We Are Known, A Spirituality of Education*, "I not only pursue truth, but truth pursues me, I not only grasp truth but truth grasps me. I not only know the truth, but truth knows me. Ultimately, I do not master truth, but truth masters me." Palmer, p. 59.

Solomon sums up this process and outcome beautifully in his own words to his learners. "My son, listen *(attend)* to my words, incline your ear *(consent* and *submit)* to my sayings. Don't lose sight of my words. Let them *penetrate* deep within your heart, for they bring life and radiant health to anyone who discovers their meaning."[emphasis added][15]

*Life* and *radiant health* are the outcomes of authentic biblical learning.

**Life and radiant health are the outcomes of authentic biblical learning.**

[15] Prov. 4:20-22, (AMP, NLT). All three meanings *attend, consent, and submit*, are resident in the Hebrew words listen and incline in verse 20. Unfortunately, the depth of meaning is lost in the simple English word listen. Additionally, the Hebrew word ear (*ozen*) as an organ of hearing is much more than a receptor of auditory sounds. The ear is to become the *receiver of divine revelation*. To uncover the ear to reveal is the equivalent to letting the words spoken by Solomon "penetrate deep within your heart." It is apparent therefore that there must be a *willingness* to learn *in such a manner* on the part of the learner. The basis for biblical hearing is for the learner to have a genuine *relationship* with Jesus Christ. He said, "I am the way, the truth, and the life. No one can come to the Father except through me." (John 14:6). The *person* of Yeshua (Jesus) and the gift of *His* Holy Spirit become the source and guide for receiving truth. Also, see Isa. 50:4-5.

CHAPTER 2

# Rediscovering a Radically New and Refreshing Way of Thinking and Living

*Many* of our commonly accepted ways of thinking and living can trap us, hinder us, and obscure the real pathways that lead to a genuine quality of life. We are all products of the cultures where we have been born and raised. Helplessly, most of us are required to live, it seems, at a laser pace while becoming engulfed along with everyone else in a technoculture world. Knowledge in all areas has exploded. We are all members of the N-Gen (internet generation). Scarcely do any of us have time to catch our breath anymore, let alone reflect on the direction we are going. The goal of parenting is to impart to our children the legacy of our hearts. But how can parents successfully do this unless they have first been able to chart a meaningful course for themselves? Who has time for contemplation while grabbing a latte from a drive-thru between errands and events?

**How can parents successfully impart the legacy of their hearts to children unless they first have been able to chart a meaningful course for themselves?**

The pressures of daily living and the influence of our culture have left parents pursuing uncertain goals while losing any real quality of life. Twenty-first-century America has no stomach for truth and righteous behavior. Our culture is tragically ignorant and even at enmity with the absolutes that God has revealed in His word. Moral relativism is the reigning god of modern culture. The fruit of this combination of ignorance and moral relativism is producing a massive ethical crisis that afflicts society everywhere, especially and sadly, our children.

The media has turned family relationships upside down as parents are ridiculed for actively overseeing their children. Popular TV shows portray students laughing about cheating at school or lying to parents. The media's message to youth is that they can only have friends if they wear the latest fashions and have the newest smartphone. Shallow data-based friendships are replacing relationships built on intimacy and companionship. If this is true, then the highest learning potentials in our children's lives may be thwarted.

Currently, our entire governmental and educational system has a dangerously skewed paradigm that, to a great extent, has excluded parents. The widespread public education theme is "save the children." Training and education are perceived to be in the hands of the "professional educators" in preschool learning centers and beyond, and governmental agencies. The implication is that everyone *except* the parents is more qualified to teach their children.

Self-centered parents have embraced the spawn-and-pawn theory of parenting (spawn them then pawn them off on others). Parents now function as broodstock. They deposit their bottle-fed babies in kiddie-care covens and school cells, keep them in Reeboks, straighten their teeth, and call it child-raising.[16]

This approach is not the original plan. It is not working. It will not work. The church has yet to seriously grapple with this truth as well, by switching its focus to equipping parents to help them fulfill their calling rather than subtly usurping the parental role in this crucial God-given task.

To combat the cultural pressures of our day, radical transformation is needed in the manner of parents' thinking. Indeed, parents are the primary educators in the lives of their children.[17] *A process of renewal must originate in the hearts and lives of parents.*

This process begins by distinguishing the vast difference between Greek and Hebraic mindsets—the Greek system of knowledge in contrast with the attitudes toward life held in Hebraic thought. Understanding the difference between the Greco-Roman and Hebraic mindset provides the threshold to reclaim authentic wholehearted learning.

The Greek approach to learning is the basis of the educational system in our culture today—absorbing information. Besides ABC's, math, and science, education is most often limited to

---

16 Dave Simmons, *Dad the Family Mentor* (Wheaton, IL: Victor Books, 1992), p. 17.

17 Simmons, *Dad the Family Mentor*, p. 11. In his Forward to Simmons' book, Howard G. Hendricks, Chairman, Center of Christian Learning, writes, "The church has our children for 1 percent of their week, school another 16 percent. The rest falls on us; the home environment we provide; the time we give."

abstract concepts or theoretical principles. Teaching focuses on the transference of knowledge.

The underlying Greco-Roman philosophy of "head learning" has shaped our attitudes toward life, formed our prevailing worldview, and even lead to many of our religious misconceptions of the God of the Bible. These prevalent influences have been at work for centuries. Such influences are tough to break. To get to the truth, one must chisel through layers of crusty fallacy created over centuries. Unlearning false preconceptions is more difficult than learning the truth at the outset.

The Greco-Roman concept of learning is the mere acquisition of knowledge only with the mind's eye. In contrast, the Hebraic view of learning embraces the whole person, resulting in "whole sight."

Hebraic learning penetrates to the heart, is deposited in the mind, and affects behavior. Knowledge and wisdom are related concepts. Both are rooted in God, and both share in the application of learning to practical living. The Hebraic idea of knowledge thus embraces *the whole human personality* rather than just the mind.

In Hebrew thought to "know" something was to experience it, rather than to intellectualize it. In Hebrew, the verb *yada* (to "know") essentially means: (1) to know by observing and reflecting (thinking), and (2) to know by experience.[18] The original meaning of "to know" someone was to share an intimate personal relationship with that one. *Yada* means to encounter, experience, and share in an intimate way.[19] Thus, a man may "know" a woman through sexual intercourse (Gen. 4:1,17, 25), and a woman may "know" a man (Num. 31:17). In biblical Hebrew, the verb *yada* denotes "an act involving concern, inner engagement, dedication, or attachment

---

[18] Gilbertson. Definition from *Vine's Expository Dictionary of Biblical Words*.

[19] Marvin R. Wilson, *Our Father Abraham* (Grand Rapids, Michigan: Wm. B. Eerdmans, 1989), 288.

to a person. It also means to have sympathy, pity, or affection for someone."[20]

Characteristically the *heart* plays a vital role in knowing. To "know" within the Hebraic worldview involves the whole person. It is much deeper than the limited cognitive transference of knowledge in the intellectual and technical areas as practiced by the Greeks.

**The heart plays a vital role in *knowing* in the Hebraic view of learning.**

A closer study of the verb *yada,* which includes the meanings "to teach," to "instruct," and to "lead," also demonstrates both cognitive and affective elements instead of knowledge. In 2 Chronicles 23:13, the same verb is used for singers of musical instruments who "lead" or "give signals for" songs of praise. Again "to know" or to "teach" went beyond mere intellectual activity; it was *to act.* Such "knowing" signifies a concrete action performed by the body rather than simply using the mind.[21]

Since the Hebraic idea of knowledge embraced the whole personality, merely grasping information was not enough. It also implied a response in the practical domain of life—in behavior and

---

20 Abraham J. Heschel, *The Prophets* (New York: Harper & Row, 1962), 57.

21 Wilson, *Our Father Abraham,* 288.

morals.[22] In Jeremiah 22:15-16, the prophet taught that knowledge was *action* or *involved concern* for another. To know God is to do justice and righteousness and to be concerned for the cause of the needy. Out of an intimate relationship with God, "knowing" results in social action and good character.

Thus, for the Hebrew learner or student, learning was meant to be *learning with a difference*. Education was tied to the holiness[23] of life, whereas for the Greeks, teaching focused on the transference of knowledge. "The Greeks learned to comprehend. The result of Hebraic learning was to revere."[24]

Yet another very marked difference existed between those who were considered "learners" in Hebrew and Greek cultures. In ancient Greek society, only the wealthy and leisure classes enjoyed the privilege of enlightenment through education. *School*

---

[22] Ibid.

[23] The concept of holiness is often confusing and usually filled with religious misconceptions. Simply stated, to *be holy is to move into God's sphere of being*. God's inward character as revealed in the law of God and expressed in the life of Jesus (the Word become flesh) was totally good and entirely without evil. Holiness is that which is separate from all that is sinful and profane. We are consecrated and become devoted to God through our trust in Him. We thus become His possession and belong to Him. It is because of our *union* with Him that we become separate or distinct from the world. As the Holy Spirit writes His laws on our hearts we too, *practically* enter into God's sphere of being by sharing His inward likeness. This happens as God's laws are written in our hearts by the Holy Spirit. We are to become clean and free of all moral pollution. So, the realm of the holy is distinct from the world with its imperfections, but we certainly live within the world. The integrity of this holiness is established and preserved *in our lives* as we walk in God's loving instructions. (see chapters 4-8). He calls us to holiness resembling His own as we become partakers of Him, sharing His inward likeness, having clean and pure thoughts, and by expressing moral integrity and love in our relationships with others. He himself has said, "You must be holy because I am holy." (1 Pet.1:16, Lev. 19:1-2, Lev. 20:7-8).

[24] Abraham J. Heschel, *Insecurity of Freedom*, (New York: Schocken Books, 1972), 41.

and *scholar* in the English language derive from the Greek verb *scholazo*, "to have leisure," "to have spare time," "to have nothing to do." Thus, a "school" (Greek *scholé*) means "leisure employed in learning."[25] Interestingly, there is no such counterpart for this Greek word in Hebrew.

The Greek worldview also regarded manual labor as degrading and those engaged in it as inferior people who were unworthy and incapable of education. Education was reserved for an elite group among the Greeks. Hebraic education was for *all* people and was for the *whole person.*

The pronounced differences between the Hebrew and Greek attitudes toward life and the concept of knowledge reveal a vast difference in worldviews, hence in the whole approach to learning. Norman Snaith sums up this radical difference in his book, *The Distinctive Ideas of the Old Testament.* "The object and aim of the Hebrew system are *da'ath Elohim* (Knowledge of God). The object and aim of the Greek system is *gnothi seauton* (Know thyself). They are poles apart in attitude and method. The Hebrew system starts with God. True wisdom is knowledge of God. 'The fear of God is the beginning of wisdom.' The result is that man can never know himself, what he is, and what is his relation to the world unless first he learns of God and becomes submissive to God's sovereign will. The Greek system, in contrast, starts from the knowledge of man, and seeks to rise to an understanding of the ways and Nature of God through the understanding of what is called 'man's higher nature.' According to the Bible, man has no higher nature except he is born of the Spirit."[26]

The approach of the Greeks to learning is nowhere in the Bible. The whole Bible, Old and New Testaments, is based on the Hebraic

---

25 Wilson, *Our Father Abraham*, 290.

26 Norman H. Snaith, *The Distinctive Ideas of the Old Testament* (New York: Schocken Books, 1964), 184-185.

approach of "knowing" God and living in His wisdom. The goal of authentic biblical learning is to acquire wisdom, which is the canon of eternally true principles that explain reality and govern morality. As a learner enters a trusting, inquisitive, and searching relationship with a loving and caring God to discover, understand, and *do*[27] the truth, such knowledge is generously revealed. Good character and social action result from "knowing" God and faithfully walking in His ways. Authentic biblical learning internalizes wisdom and truth in the learner's heart and displays itself in a useful and fruitful lifestyle. The goal of learning, therefore, is to acquire wholehearted wisdom that transforms the character and alters lifestyles rather than the dull and often boring exercise of merely assimilating mental knowledge as an end in itself.

**The goal of learning is to acquire wholehearted wisdom that transforms the character and alters lifestyles.**

---

27 The *moral* conditions of spiritual knowledge are continually insisted on. "Anyone who wants *to do* the will of God *will know* whether my teaching is from God or is merely my own." (John 7:17, italics are mine). Once again it is clear that authentic biblical learning occurs when there is both a willing desire to learn truth and a heart to test its reality by putting what is learned into practice (obedience).

Authentic biblical learning leads to a lifetime of adventure and discovery that produces personal wholeness and fulfillment.[28]

I wonder what expression you would see on the face of any educator today if you asked, "Is your number one priority with your students the pursuit of wholehearted wisdom?" A majority would likely not understand your question! A Greek learning mindset locks the learner out of the priceless discovery of truth and reality

---

[28] R. Laird Harris, Gleason L. Archer, Jr., Bruce K. Waltke, *Theological Wordbook of the Old Testament* (Chicago: Moody Bible Institute, 1980), 930-931. Perhaps the one Hebrew word that most beautifully describes this fulfillment and ultimate outcome of authentic biblical learning is the word *shalom*. The general meaning behind the root *sh-l-m* is of completion and fulfillment—of entering into a state of wholeness and unity, a restored relationship. Inherent also in the meaning is the concept of peace being restored through payment. Recompense for sin, either national or personal, must be given. Once that obligation has been met, wholeness is restored. Implicit in *shalom* is the idea of *unimpaired* relationships with others and *fulfillment* in one's undertakings. Shalom is the result of God's activity in covenant (*b'rit*) and is the result of righteousness (Isa. 32:17). In nearly two-thirds of its occurrences, *shalom* describes the state of fulfillment which is the result of God's presence. This is specifically indicated in those references to the "covenant of peace" (*b'rit shalom*, Mal. 2:5, Ezek. 34:24-26) with His chosen representatives. This sort of peace has its source in God. He is the one who will speak *shalom* to His people. His promise to David in 1 Chron. 22:9-10 puts *shalom* in context with *m'nuha* "calmness, "*nuah* "rest," and *sheqet* "to be quiet," as these are gifts from God. The classic statement of this concept is the Aaronic benediction (Num. 6:24-26) which identifies the man to whom God has given *shalom* as the one who is blessed (*barak*), guarded (*shamar*), and treated graciously *(hanan*), by Yahweh. This is fulfillment through the divine gift. There is also a strong eschatological element present in the meaning of *shalom*. Messiah, "David's greater son," is specifically identified as the Prince of Peace (*sar shalom*—the one who brings fulfillment and righteousness to the earth. Paul (Eph. 2:14) links these themes in his identification of Christ as our peace. He is the messianic prince who brings wholeness, but He is also God's last word—the "concluding sacrifice" that brings redemption to mankind. This *shalom is God's goal for His learners*! And this will be the outcome of authentic biblical learning: wholeness, soundness, health, restored relationships, peace, fulfillment in one's undertakings, and safety. These are the fruits (results or outcomes) of pursuing, receiving, and living in wisdom.

revealed to the learners who choose to walk within the parameters of Hebraic learning or authentic biblical learning.

Wisdom pursues and searches for those who would become authentic biblical learners. Wisdom shouts in the streets!

Chapter 3

# Wisdom Cries Out

Wisdom **SHOUTS** in the street,
Hear as understanding raises her voice!
She stands on the hilltop and at the crossroads.
At the entrance to the city, at the city gates,
she cries aloud,
"I call to you, to all of you! I am raising
my voice to all people.
How naive you are!
Let me give you common sense.
O foolish ones let me give you understanding.
Listen to me! For I have excellent things to tell you.
Everything I say is right, for I speak the truth
and hate every kind of deception.
My advice is wholesome and good.
There is nothing crooked or twisted in it.
My words are plain to anyone with understanding,
clear to those who want to learn.[29]
– *Solomon*

***Wisdom*** cries out at the thoroughfares of every person's life. But what is wisdom? Who is listening?

---

29 Prov. 8:1-9.

Wisdom searches for parents who will give welcome entrance to instruction and discipline in their own lives first. Authentic biblical learning begins with parents. Parents, in turn, create an environment that stimulates the natural desire for every child to learn wisdom.

There are substantial rewards for the learner of wisdom.[30] Consider for a moment the benefits that are the result of the attainment of wisdom:

### *the outstanding rewards of wisdom*

---

***1 Happy is the person who finds wisdom and gains understanding.***
***2 The profit of wisdom is better than silver, and her wages are better than gold.***
***3 Wisdom is more precious than rubies; nothing you desire can compare with her.***
***4 She offers you life in her right hand, and riches and honor in her left.***
***5 She will guide you down delightful paths; all her ways are satisfying.***
***6 Wisdom is a tree of life to those who embrace her; happy are those who hold her tightly.***

---

[30] Prov. 3:13-18. Also see Proverbs chapter 8.

With wisdom's rewards so high, one might logically conclude that not only would the search for wisdom be considered one of the most worthwhile pursuits by every person but that it would be the centerpiece of any educational system as well. However, the implication from the words of Solomon, one of the wisest men known ever to live in world history,[31] is that wisdom itself searches for an audience in a boisterous world where few are listening. Wisdom summons would-be learners. Wisdom cries out amid everyone's pursuits, in public gathering places, business centers, the malls of America and Wall Street, and in the public policy decision centers of cities, states, and our nation, including Washington, DC ("at the entrance to the gates of the city"). To everyone comes the same question, *"How long, O naive (simple) ones, will you love simplicity? And scoffers delight themselves in scoffing, and fools hate knowledge?"*

But who is listening?

[31] "God gave Solomon great wisdom and understanding, and knowledge too vast to be measured. In fact, his wisdom exceeded that of all the wise men of the East and the wise men of Egypt. He was wiser than anyone else, including Ethan the Ezrahite and Heman, Calcol, and Darda—the sons of Mahol. His fame spread throughout all the surrounding nations. He composed some 3,000 proverbs and wrote 1,005 songs. He could speak with authority about all kinds of plants, from the great cedar of Lebanon to the tiny hyssop that grows from cracks in a wall. He could also speak about animals, birds, reptiles, and fish. And kings from every nation sent their ambassadors to listen to the wisdom of Solomon." (I King 4:29-34).

**The implication from the words of one of the wisest men ever known to live in world history is that wisdom itself searches for an audience in a boisterous world where few are listening.**

Solomon's world was much like our society and culture of today. The highest public acclaim and adoration is bestowed on today's societal kings and queens, from the NFL to the big screen, especially those who publicly defy traditional or godly values. In contrast, those individuals who are proponents for wise and moral principles are mocked and scorned from Capitol Hill to the classroom.

Our culture seems to have swallowed the campaign lie during presidential races; namely, that character does not matter. All that counts are the "issues." This sleight of hand has become remarkably deceitful and intensely powerful in the thoughts of individuals. Anyone voicing legitimate concern for moral decency in any realm is quickly labeled as hateful and politically incorrect, and his opinion discarded. Language has been raped, while truth has been rejected and obscured.

None of us enjoy a rebuke—either from a friend or enemy. We do not care for an assessment of ourselves that strikes us any lower than our own opinion of ourselves. Yet the first learning threshold for authentic biblical learning can only be crossed by personal and genuine acceptance of Solomon's accurate assessment of us as prospective students. *Naive* or *simple (fool),*[32] describes the group in which we all must first enroll. In this class of learners, unwise students are "fools" (Prov. 1:7) or "simple ones" (Prov. 1:22). To be clear, fool or simple one is not to be confused with a mentally defective person. In wisdom literature, the different kinds of fools, both young and old, are "the raw material on which the teacher had to work, and they represent varying degrees of rawness."[33] The books of wisdom literature include Job, Psalms, Proverbs, Ecclesiastes, and Song of Solomon. These five books deal precisely with our human struggles and real-life experiences. Perhaps as much as anything else, the term fool is descriptive of an attitude, bent of mind, or direction in life which needs correcting.[34] Scripture uses this word regarding *moral* rather than intellectual deficiencies. The "fool" is not so much one lacking in mental powers, as one who misuses them, not one who does not reason, but reasons wrongly.[35]

**The term fool is descriptive of an attitude, bent of mind, or direction in life which needs correcting.**

---

32 The whole world is spiritually corrupt and displays a general disregard of God. In a sense, therefore, when we take all of Scripture into consideration, all human beings—in one way or another—are fools. See 1 Kings 8:46, Ps.14:1-3, 130:3, Rom. 3:10-18, and 1 Cor. 1:18-25.

33 John Patterson, *The Wisdom of Israel* (Nashville: Abingdon Press, 1961), 64.

34 Wilson, *Our Father Abraham*, 283.

35 Gilbertson, From *New Unger's Bible Dictionary*.

There is a spectrum of meanings in the Hebrew language for a fool, which occurs more than 100 times in the book of Proverbs. The *open* fool is translated as "simple" and comes from the Hebrew term *peti.* The prologue to the book of Proverbs speaks of giving prudence to the simple.[36] In this instance, the one who is naive (simple) is *open-minded and open-hearted.* Such a learner is accessible and will welcome instruction and correction from a wise man. Though often immature, inexperienced, and easily led into all kinds of enticement, the *peti* is, fortunately, teachable. A "simple" one might be naive, gullible, and easily fooled,[37] yet his mind remains open to the entrance of wisdom. This openness has the potential of being turned into virtue as quickly as a vice.[38] Because this one is naïve and inexperienced, he can be taught to get into mischief, as easily as he can be taught to do the right thing.

The words *kesil* and *ewil* refer to the second kind of fool that the wise teacher of wisdom encountered. The basic idea behind both these Hebrew terms seems to be similar, namely, "thickness" or "fatness." The notion of thickness suggests a hardened, sluggish, and obstinate person, a person who is thickheaded or dense in the sense of *moral deficiency.* The *kesil* is so self-confident that he is set in his ways. As a dog returns to its vomit, so a fool (*kesil*)[39] repeats his folly. He despises instruction,[40] is contentious,[41] strong-willed, and refuses to learn readily. Hence this learner is characterized by his propensity to disregard moral ideals. He finds pleasure in doing

---

36 See Prov. 1:4 and 1:22.

37 See Prov. 7:7.

38 Wilson, *Our Father Abraham*, 284.

39 Prov. 26:11.

40 Prov. 1:22, 18:2.

41 Prov. 18:6.

evil[42] and brings bitterness and grief to his parents.[43] In sum, he rejects the fear of the Lord.[44]

Teachers of wisdom also confronted the *letz*. This word means "scoffer" or "scorner." The *letz* is a *mocker*. With arrogant superiority, he ridicules all that is good and holy. In modern Hebrew, the word for "clown," *letzan,* is derived from the same root. The *letz* knows all the answers, turns his back to wisdom, and hates correction.[45]

The final word for fool is *nabal.* Devoid of spiritual perception, the *nabal* has a *closed mind* to the "God-idea." The fool (*nabal*) says in his heart, "there is no God."[46] In his arrogance, the *nabal* is characterized by an attitude that fails to reckon with God. Such a fool negates the foundational presupposition of Scripture, "In the beginning God…" (Gen. 1:1). The prophet Isaiah indicates that this impiety of the *nabal* also includes *moral depravity* (he is "busy with evil") and *social insensitivity* ("the hungry he leads empty, and from the thirsty he withholds water.") If one's theology is faulty, one's spiritual and social consciousness is blunted. Through vile deeds, the fool states, as it were, that the living reality of God is missing from human experience. But his viewpoint is spiritually defective. In his scorn, he fails to acknowledge God for who He is. In so doing, the *nabal* declares himself to be a "God-denying" fool.[47]

It may be helpful to visualize the spectrum of a fool, as illustrated on the following continuum.

---

42 Prov. 10:23.

43 Prov. 10:1, 17:21, 25.

44 Prov. 1:29.

45 Prov. 9:7-8.

46 Ps 14:1.

47 Wilson, *Our Father Abraham*, p. 287.

***peti:*** **teachable, morally sensitive, aware of God, open minded and heart**

***kesil / ewil:*** **thick headed, morally hardened (thick hearted)**

***letz:*** **mocker**

***nabal:*** **unteachable, morally depraved, God denying, closed mind and heart**

*moral receptivity of the types of fools with decreasing ability to receive and apply wisdom*

In sum, all four descriptive words for fool underscore the fact that the nature of authentic biblical learning addresses heart issues, not just the intellect. Every type of fool has a bent (moral receptivity and disposition). In each category, the disposition of a fool requires transformation and wisdom.

When Adam sinned in the garden, we lost both our *moral* likeness and the *wisdom* of God. One of the original Hebrew words for sin is *het*, which is a term from the world of archery or marksmanship conveying the idea of "falling short." It means to miss the mark or fall short of a target, in the same way, an arrow or slingshot misses the bull's-eye.[48] Authentic biblical education is wholehearted education for the whole person, which, by its very substance, contents, and power, will transform the moral character and impart wisdom to *willing* learners.

As shown in the continuum of the fool above, one can readily observe that each of the four types of fools (the *peti, kesil* or *ewil, letz, and nabal*) could all have equally outstanding IQs or intellect. Yet the internal bent of the four fools is worlds apart. The *peti* learner (open-minded fool) is teachable and will profit greatly from instruction and discipline. Thick headed and thick hearted describes the *kesil/ewil* leaner who is morally hardened. A *letz* learner is characterized as a mocker. The *nabal* learner (closed-minded fool) does not incline to learn whatsoever. His bent (inner attitude of pride and rebellion) excludes him from learning and seals his continued folly (failure in life). In summary, the term *fool* is descriptive of an attitude, bent of mind, or direction in life which needs correcting.

Wisdom is the daily ability to successfully meet the myriad of challenges along the road of life. Authentic biblical instruction imparts wisdom primarily in the practical realm, not the theoretical. True wisdom offers practical guidance that teaches people how to apply divine truth to daily life. Wisdom provides skillful advice and discipline in solving current problems common to the human condition. Wisdom is not found at the top of the graduate school mountain but in the sandpile, at home.

Solomon, as a teacher of wisdom, had one consuming desire regarding fools of whatever stripe: to drive out the folly and teach wisdom. He had learned well from his father, David. His father was a king, warrior, and administrator who had no equal before or after in him in Israel. King David was a person of integrity and measureless abilities. Though David committed murder and

---

48 See I Kings 8:46 and Judges 20:16.

fornication, his repentance restored his relationship with God. David's failure is instructive for us as parents. Even with his failures, he is referred to as being perfect (1 Kings 15:3)! How can this be?

King David had a heart that was not morally perfect, but a heart that was perfect *toward God*. Perfection does not mean a sinless, flawless heart. The basic definition of perfect is completeness, maturity. In David's life, we see fully displayed the goal of wholehearted education—completeness, and maturity. His trust in and his heart *toward God* was the reason David could be called perfect. I Kings 15:5 goes on to say, "David did what was right in the sight of the Lord, and did not deviate from anything that He commanded him all the days of his life, except in the case of Uriah the Hittite."

World history archives this record of King David with these words, "So he shepherded them according to the integrity of his heart and guided them by the discernment and skillfulness which controlled his hands."[49]

As the creator, God created a world that runs by absolute laws that exist apart from humans and our space/time continuum. God created a world consisting of physical properties (matter and energy) governed by laws of physics, a spirit world (angels), *and* a world of human life guided by moral principles with right and wrong behavior leading to positive and inevitable consequences. Wisdom will convey the way the world is and the way it works. Wisdom will unveil the truth regarding the mysteries of the spiritual world. And wisdom will reveal the moral and ethical laws that God established to govern human relationships. God, Himself is the source who reveals the real and unchangeable principles

---

[49] (NAS) and (AMP), Ps. 78:72.

for three-dimensional living in the truth and the realities of His world.[50] God is completely trustworthy!

The fundamental basis for understanding truth and reality comes when we establish a real relationship with Jesus Christ. In John 14:6, He said, "I am the way, the truth, and the life." Wisdom is graciously given to the learner first through a trusting relationship with Jesus Christ. It also comes from our persistent requests as His children. "If you need wisdom, if you want to know what God wants you to do, ask him, and he will gladly tell you. He will not resent you're asking."[51] Wisdom is revealed through the indwelling presence of the Holy Spirit in the learner and the gift

---

[50] Listen as wisdom calls out! Hear as understanding raises her voice! "The LORD formed me from the beginning, before he created anything else. I was appointed in ages past, at the very first, before the earth began. I was born before the oceans were created, before the springs bubbled forth their waters. Before the mountains and the hills were formed, I was born before he had made the earth and fields and the first handfuls of soil. "I was there when he established the heavens, when he drew the horizon on the oceans. I was there when he set the clouds above, when he established the deep fountains of the earth. I was there when he set the limits of the seas, so they would not spread beyond their boundaries. And when he marked off the earth's foundations, I was the architect at his side. I was his constant delight, rejoicing always in his presence. And how happy I was with what he created—his wide world and all the human family! "And so, my children, listen to me, for happy are all who follow my ways. Listen to my counsel and be wise. Don't ignore it. "Happy are those who listen to me, watching for me daily at my gates, waiting for me outside my home! For whoever finds me finds life and wins approval from the LORD. But those who miss me have injured themselves. All who hate me love death." Prov 8:1, 22-36 (NLT).

[51] James 1:5 (NLT).

of God's revelation of *Himself* in the Scriptures.[52] And wisdom is imparted through fathers and mothers to their children.[53]

Wisdom is readily available. But you cannot force-feed wisdom.[54]

Wisdom calls out to the naive or simple (all fools) with an invitation to learn wisdom. Authentic biblical learning requires a *diligent search for wisdom.* Wisdom is the canon of eternally true principles that explain reality and govern morality. The call to be a learner of wisdom comes with a promise of immense reward. For those who will listen, wisdom offers a *pathway to life, ways of pleasantness,* and *paths of peace* for the entire family, beginning with the parents.

---

52 These are the proverbs of Solomon, David's son, king of Israel. The purpose of these proverbs is to teach people wisdom and discipline, and to help them understand wise sayings. Through these proverbs, people will receive instruction in discipline, good conduct, and doing what is right, just, and fair. These proverbs will make the simpleminded clever. They will give knowledge and purpose to young people. Let those who are wise listen to these proverbs and become even wiser. And let those who understand receive guidance by exploring the depth of meaning in these proverbs, parables, wise sayings, and riddles. Fear of the LORD is the beginning of knowledge. Only fools despise wisdom and discipline. Prov 1:1-7 (NLT).

53 {A Father's Exhortation: Acquire Wisdom} Listen, my child, to what your father teaches you. Don't neglect your mother's teaching. Prov 1:8 (NLT).

54 My words are plain to anyone with understanding, clear to those *who want to learn*. Prov. 8:9 (NLT).

# Part 2
# Parents First

## Chapter 4

# Parents First

## The Starting Point

**Wisdom** must first be planted, then rooted, in parents. Authentic and real foundations for biblical education begin in the subterranean soil of the hearts of Mom and Dad. These foundations will find practical expression in the lifestyle of the parents as well. If parents desire the development of character, fruitful living, and achievement in the lives of their children, they must start with themselves.[55]

There are two sides to parenthood. What we *are* and what we *do*. Our character *and* behavior matter more than any particular "parenting techniques." Children do what we do, not what we say.

Children play with our words but work off our hearts. Solomon sums up the essential focus, "Keep your heart with all vigilance, and above all that you guard, for out of it flow the springs of life."[56] What is in our hearts ultimately controls our actions. What is

---

55 The essence of authentic biblical education begins with parents, *not* children. Children learn best by what they see demonstrated, *then* taught by their own parents. Notice this order in Deut 6:6-7, "And *you must commit yourselves wholeheartedly to these commands* I am giving you today. *(Then)* Repeat them again and again to your children. Talk about them when you are at home and when you are away on a journey, when you are lying down and when you are getting up again. (NLT)

56 Prov 4:23 (AMP).

expressed from parents' hearts and demonstrated in the daily crucible of family life is of incalculable consequence to the well-being, development, academic prowess, achievement, and life fulfillment of their children.

The home is the foundational institution for wholehearted education, with the children studying their parents' lives as the curriculum. The parents' curriculum emerges from the foundation of God's character and instructions imprinted in their hearts and expressed in their everyday lifestyle. The home provides an environment that, for better or worse, becomes the incubator of a child's love for God, himself, and his neighbor.

Properly nurtured, this planted love roots itself in the hearts of children, which in turn becomes the basis for personal wholeness, lawful social behavior, productive citizenship, and a lifetime of achievement. These fruitful outcomes flow from the loving heart of a righteous and tenderhearted God. All He has said and done demonstrates His constant desire for man to enjoy the highest possible fulfillment in life.

The profound simplicity of the fact the home is the foundational center of learning has become obscured by the complicated array of educational efforts, programs, and experimental initiatives that are currently used within our school systems, often failing at all ages and levels of education.

Just as there is a starting square in the game of Monopoly, there is a starting point to life and learning—HOME. As in Monopoly, most of the educational enterprise in today's culture endeavors to purchase Boardwalk while failing to begin at START.

We are living in a day of tragic ethical crisis. Gun violence by students in schools continues to bring heartbreak to parents and grip our nation. Failure abounds inside and outside the classroom. Teen depression and suicide have reached record levels. Social media has produced unprecedented levels of peer pressure causing low self-esteem and insecurity, which can spiral into depression and even suicide. These tragedies are incurring within all learning environments and reveal the depth of the learning dysfunctions in our culture today. Confusion is rampant. Our society is tragically ignorant and even at enmity with the existence of God as He reveals Himself in the Scriptures and His commandments.

Yet, there is an answer to relativism, secularism, and ignorance, which are all contributing to the moral and educational failures that are endemic in our society. Recovering and understanding the application of God's eternal character and will for His people, as revealed in His loving law, lead to dynamic solutions for this crisis.

Every day, headlines underscore the two choices facing our failing educational approaches: GO TO JAIL or return to START. There is a choice. Parents can either choose to place the primary responsibility for educating their children on others outside the home or choose to accept the challenge of becoming the first instructors of their children at home. Biblical principles for parents to prepare children for learning and living are becoming exceedingly urgent.

In biblical history, we rediscover the mystery of the Magna Carta (The Great Charter) of education. The nation of Israel had just escaped bondage from Egypt. They had escaped tyranny as slaves for more than 400 years to become a free nation. Moses, their leader, unveiled the foundation of how their life of freedom was to be established. Moses was a mere spokesman for God who had authored their escape from Egyptian bondage and disclosed a new way of life. God desired nothing but the best for Israel.

After first receiving the Ten Commandments, in Deuteronomy chapter 6, Moses then presents the Magna Charta to parents for authentic biblical learning. This foundational directive mandates parents to be the first and foremost educators of their children. It is a summons to a clean and enduring fear of God and wholehearted commitment to His commandments. This directive was given to preserve and usher in the greatest quality of life for every family and the nation as a whole.

The summons in Deuteronomy 6:1-9 comes with a promise of great reward to the parents: "*These are all the commands, laws, and regulations that the LORD your God told me to teach you so you may obey them in the land you are about to enter and occupy, and so you and your children and grandchildren might fear the LORD your God as long as you live. If you obey all his laws and commands, you will enjoy a long life. Listen closely, Israel, to everything I say. Be careful to obey. Then all will go well with you, and you will have many children in the land flowing with milk and honey, just as the LORD, the God of your ancestors, promised you. 'Hear, O Israel! The LORD is our God, the LORD alone. And you must love the LORD your God with all your heart, all your soul, and all your strength.' And* ***you must commit yourselves wholeheartedly to these commands I am giving you today****. Repeat them again and again to your children. Talk about them when you are at home and when you are away on a journey, when you are lying down and when you are getting up again. Tie them to your hands as a reminder and wear them on your forehead. Write them on the doorposts of your house and on your gates.*" [emphasis added]

Solomon's diligent search to understand the meaning of life led him to write, "*Here is my final conclusion: Fear God and obey his commands, for this is the whole (duty) of every person.*"[57] In this verse, the Hebrew meaning of duty goes far beyond an obligation. The true biblical meaning of duty is that the fear of God and obedience to His commands are the original purpose for man's whole being.

---

[57] Eccles. 12:13. Solomon's search for finding the meaning in life is documented in the book of Ecclesiastes. As pointed out earlier (see Chapter 3, footnote 30) Solomon was noted to be the wisest man ever to live. After exploring the vast array of natural sciences, educational disciplines, pleasures, and every possible source for finding satisfaction in his life, he arrived at this conclusion.

Encapsulated in this saying of Solomon is the whole of man, the central and entire purpose for his being, without regard to being rich or poor, or to any rank or social status.

Seven weeks after their liberation from slavery, the Israelites found themselves at the foot of Mount Sinai, where the world was changed forever.

*They met God!*

Undoubtedly, intense fear gripped the Israelites as they gathered at the foot of Mt. Sinai as the awe-inspiring presence of their Holy God erupted from His dwelling place in the heavens and touched the top of the mountain. The magnitude of this event was like an earthquake and a raging fire. At the foot of Mt. Sinai, nearly one million people became engulfed in an ear-deafening, eye-blinding, ground-shaking event that made their hearts tremble.[58] Just imagine yourself in the same situation. The ground is unsteady under your feet, and you become engulfed in a shroud of midnight blackness except for fire blazing from the top of Sinai to the very heavens.[59] And then you hear the thundering voice of God.

Mount Sinai had disappeared in smoke. The LORD had descended on it in the form of fire. The smoke billowed into the sky like smoke from a furnace, and the whole mountain shook with a violent earthquake. As the horn blast grew louder and louder, Moses spoke, and God thundered His reply.[60] The God of Israel spoke His commandments for all to hear.

For the first time in recorded human history, rules were written down based on absolute right and wrong. In the Ten Commandments, specific acts, behavior, and even inner attitudes towards the living God and fellow men were clearly defined as being fundamentally right or wrong. These laws/instructions

---

[58] Exod. 19:16.

[59] Deut. 4:11.

[60] Exod. 19:18-19.

remain, even if people try to change (or deny) them. The Ten Commandments were given to an entire people and disclosed an absolute morality rather than a social consensus. At Sinai, God set out to create a community where ordinary people, not saints, would reinforce each other's efforts to do the right thing. Israel was to be a model society where doing good was not intended to be an unusual and heroic choice by a unique individual, but *just the way people do things.* To worship the only true God and to follow His directions to the Israelites was to live as human beings were intended to live—a life of wholeness, security, well-being, and accomplishment.

God, unlike any other deity in the history of man, manifested Himself and spoke to His people. God's presence was unmistakable and real. Fear gripped the Israelites because of being in the presence of Yahweh.[61] All of Israel experienced the fear of

[61] Yahweh (the LORD) is the *personal name* of God who made Himself known to all of Israel at Sinai. This personal name of God occurs 5321 times in the Old Testament. Yahweh was unlike any other God. God's name identifies *His nature*, so that a request for His "name" is equivalent to asking about His character. (Exod. 3:13-15) In verse 14, God's promise to Moses had been, "Certainly I will be with you" (Exod. 3:12). So His assertion in verse 14 would seem to be saying, "I am present is what I am." Indeed, the fundamental promise of His testament is, "I will be their God, and they will be my people" (Exod. 6:7 contrast with Hosea 1:9); thus "Yahweh," "faithful presence," is God's testamentary nature or name (Exod. 6:2, 4; Deuteronomy 7:9; Isaiah 26:4). The use of Yahweh as a divine name goes back to earliest times (Genesis 4:1,26; 9:26). And it is Yahweh who is immanent in Eden's revelations (Genesis 2:4-25). Yahweh, this glorious and fearful name (Deuteronomy 28:58, Leviticus 24:11-16) connotes God's *nearness*, His *concern for man*, and the *revelation of His redemptive covenant*. Only in pre-New Testament times was God's personal name replaced with the less intimate title "my master" (Heb. *adonay)* and (Gr., *kurious*) "Lord." Ultimately the connotations of the name Yahweh are fulfilled in the "covenant of peace," when the God who has been present from the first will be fully present at the last (Isaiah 41:4). Ezekiel anticipates God's "sanctuary in the midst of them forevermore" (Ezekiel 37:26) and his eschatological city's being named *YHWH shamma* "Yahweh is there." (R. Laird Harris, Gleason L. Archer, Jr.,

the Lord. They were terrified, astonished, and in awe of God. True reverence, honor, and respect were the outcomes of Israel's encounter with God. As parents, we must cultivate the same honor and respect toward God that the Israelites had at Sinai. The root of pure morality[62] in life is the *fear of God* reigning in our hearts, a reverence for God's majesty, deference to His authority, and a dread of His wrath. The standard of morality is the law of God revealed in the Scriptures. If we truly fear God as parents, we will respect all His commandments and take care to keep them.

God's tremendous love and affection for His people had already been shown by the powerful display of His might when He rescued them from the disheartening slavery they were experiencing under Pharaoh's harsh rule. Yahweh provided all they needed for their escape from Egypt. God provided their escape based solely on His grace without any merit from undeserving Israel. Understanding that all these commandments are based on the grace of God is crucial for their proper application. God's commandments did not *save* them; His commandments were designed to protect and assure the Israelites success. These blessings were conferred on His people who had already been saved from slavery.

God's Ten Commandments are His loving instructions based on the foundation of His prior love and grace.[63] If obeyed and followed, the commandments given at Mr. Sinai are designed to

---

Bruce K. Waltke, *Theological Wordbook of the Old Testament*, [Chicago, Moody Bible Institute, 1980], 210-212).

62 The proper awe, honor, and respect (fear) of God is *the* source of integrity and virtue. Ps. 19:8-9 states, "Reverence for the LORD is *pure*, lasting forever. The laws of the LORD are true; each one is fair. The commandments of the LORD are right, bringing joy to the heart. The commands of the LORD are clear, giving insight to life."

63 "I am the LORD your God, who rescued you from slavery in Egypt." Exod. 20:2 This entire action of deliverance was based on the love and grace of God.

be life-giving tributaries releasing the floodgates of the depths of His grace and love in the daily lives of God's people. God's covenant with Israel was based on the exceptional relationship He established with them. The keeping of the Ten Commandments by all the people of Israel assured the profound blessings in every aspect of their lives for every household. Each parent's response to receive and obey God's loving instructions for themselves is linked inextricably to the spiritual destiny, well-being, and life of achievement for their children (*all will go well with you*).[64]

Abraham believed God before the giving of any of the Biblical commandments, and he was commended for his faith by the Lord. His *living trust* in God was the qualifying ingredient that accounted for Abraham's righteousness in God's eyes. King David, who was a lover of God and lover of God's law, describes beautifully the sweet fragrance, joy, and well-being of those who welcome the writing of God's laws into their hearts by the Holy Spirit. As Israel's chief musician, David sang of the beauty of the Law of God. "The law of the LORD is perfect, reviving the soul. The decrees of the LORD are trustworthy, making wise the simple. The commandments of the LORD are right, bringing joy to the heart. The commands of the LORD are clear, giving insight into life. Reverence for the LORD is pure, lasting forever. The laws of the LORD are true; each one is fair. They are more desirable than gold, even the finest gold. They are sweeter than honey, even honey dripping from the comb. They are a warning to those who hear them; there is a great reward for those who obey them."[65] It was

---

64 Notice the promises for obedience. If you obey all his laws and commands, *you will enjoy a long life*. Listen closely, Israel, to everything I say. Be careful to obey. Then *all will go well with you*, and you will have many children.

65 Ps. 19:7-11.

his love for God's law that gave David the distinction of being "a man after God's own heart."[66]

The keeping of God's commandments does not produce righteousness; faith does. The observing of God's commandments produces well-being and blessing in those who believe. Most of Israel failed to enter their promised inheritance, not because they did not have the commandments, but because they refused to trust in God.

Ironically, perhaps just as many believers today have failed to enjoy many of the blessings of God and experience total well-being because they have ignored or refused to observe some of the commandments of God, even though they may have great faith within their lives. Many believers who recognize the truth that salvation is by grace alone have mistakenly given the Ten Commandments scarce if any attention.[67] How can we decry the moral relativism

---

66 The commonly held teaching within the church is that it was David's repentance after committing adultery and murder that gave him the distinction of being a man after God's own heart. Although David certainly did exhibit true repentance and a contrite spirit for these gross failures, his absolute affinity and respect for all of God's law was the reason for this commendation from God himself.

67 A commonly held misinterpretation among believers of the word "fulfill" in Matthew 5:17 has contributed to a license for the dismissal of some of God's commandments with the explanation that the "grace" of God has eliminated the need to obey ALL of his commandments. Note first of all the words of Jesus Christ himself in Matthew 5:17-19: (Teaching about the Law—) "Don't misunderstand why I have come. I did not come to abolish the law of Moses (*Torah*) or the writings of the prophets. No, I came to fulfill (complete) them. I assure you, until heaven and earth disappear, even the smallest detail of God's law will remain until its purpose is achieved. *So if you break the smallest commandment and teach others to do the same, you will be the least in the Kingdom of Heaven*. But anyone who obeys God's laws and teaches them will be great in the Kingdom of Heaven." (NLT) Unfortunately the Hebrew word "*Torah*" which literally means "teaching, doctrine," is rendered in both the Septuagint and the New Testament by the Greek word "*nomos*," which means "law." Greek has had a more direct and pervasive influence on English and other modern languages than Hebrew has, and this is why in most languages one speaks of the "Law" of Moses rather than the "Teaching"

and secularism in which we are living, if we as God's children are ignorant of God's loving instructions ourselves? A cursory glance at any daily newspaper and five minutes of watching the evening news reveals how relevant and extensive God's commandments are to healing the moral sickness of our society and providing real and lasting solutions for the issues of our day.

As parents, we must first learn to live within the borders of these loving instructions. How can we teach them if we do not know them? If we are not yet living within the discipline of these

---

of Moses. It is also part of the reason why the *Torah* has mistakenly come to be thought of by believers as legalistic in character. The Greek word *plerosai* "to fill" means "to complete." Yeshua's (Jesus' name in Hebrew and Aramaic) "fulfilling" the Torah is thought to mean that it is unnecessary for people to fulfill it now. But there is no logic to the proposition that Yeshua's obeying the Torah does away with our need to obey it. In fact, Paul, whose object in his letter to the Romans is to foster "the obedience that comes from trusting" in Yeshua, teaches that such trusting does not abolish Torah but confirms it. (See Romans 1:5 and 3:31). Yeshua kept the *Torah* perfectly. In so doing he didn't abolish the teaching of Moses (the law) but completed it. He came to *complete our understanding* of the *Torah.* In other words Yeshua did not come to abolish but "to make full" (plerosai) the meaning of what the Torah and the ethical demands require so that we can try more effectively to *be* and *do* what they say to be and do. Having stated that he has come not to abolish but complete the teaching of Moses (Matthew 5:17-19) in the remainder of chapter 5, Yeshua gives six specific cases in which he explains the fuller spiritual meaning of points in the Jewish Law. The entire theme and agenda of the Sermon on the Mount is Yeshua's teaching to make full or complete the listener's understanding so that they could more fully express what being God's people was all about. (David Stern, *Jewish New Testament Commentary*, [Maryland, Jewish New Testament Publications, 1992], pp. 25-26). The keeping of the teaching of Moses was to also be accompanied by *inner alignment and fidelity of heart* with these teachings. Finally, the keeping of God's commandments will be one of the primary characteristics of believers (saints) in the last days. John writes the following in Revelation 12:17, "Then the dragon became angry at the woman, and he declared war against the rest of her children—all who keep God's commandments and confess that they belong to Jesus. (NLT) Notice how inextricably *both* faith *and* the keeping of God's commandments are combined here.

caring instructions, how can we direct the training of our children into genuine biblical learning?

To live within the parameters of God's loving instructions keeps one under the magnificence of His favor. These words are the very imprint of the nature of God, designed to continually keep God's children living under the everflowing and marvelous lovingkindness of a holy and loving God.

The prophet Jeremiah succinctly summarizes the plan and purpose of God for a man when faith is combined with the keeping of God's law. "But this is the *new covenant* I will make with the people of Israel on that day," says the LORD. "I will put my laws in their minds, and I will write them on their hearts. I will be their God, and they will be my people."[68] God's will for us is vibrant living—from the inside out. In the new covenant, the Holy Spirit works to imprint God's loving instructions in our hearts. The laws that were written in the Tablets of Stone by the finger of God are now written in our hearts by the finger of the Holy Spirit. *The laws are the same*, except the power to keep them comes from the enabling presence of the Holy Spirit in the life of believers.

The Holy Spirit accomplishes a remarkable transformation of heart when we first enter the kingdom of God. Subsequently, the precious gift of the Holy Spirit brings an enabling strength to break and subdue the hardened rebellious spirit within each one of us. This excellent resident Spirit of God now gives the believer the *inclination* to obey these laws, *personally writes* these laws on our minds and hearts, *causes us to be familiar with them*, and *helps us care to keep* them, and *enables us to keep* them. These words, which had formerly been a code of morals, external to man and obeyed as a duty, became—through the Holy Spirit—an incredible reservoir of God's grace, shaping our character from the inside out! The presence of God within our lives gives us the *disposition for*

---

68 Jer. 31:33.

*obedience*, a holy process which, if willingly allowed to run full course within our hearts, will ultimately lead to full conformity of thought, affection, and conduct to the rules of the divine law.

We begin to recognize that within ourselves, a copy of the nature of God is being inscribed in our hearts. Rooted in God's love, our heavenly Father's goal for us as his children is to share His DNA. God's laws are a revelation of His nature and character. We are to be like *Him*!

God's laws, once embraced by parents, become *pathways of loving instruction* that flow out of the nature of God into their lives. As parents cultivate a respectful relationship with God and His caring instructions, Yahweh's goodness will be recognized and imparted into the hearts of their children as well. All of God's loving instructions are to be *received* in our hearts, *incorporated into our lifestyles*, and subsequently *taught* and *reinforced* in the lives of our children.

Once written by the finger of God in stone at Mt. Sinai, God's Ten Commandments written in the tender hearts of obedient parents by the Holy Spirit and then taught as loving instructions to their children become an unfailing moral compass. The beacon of integrity leads to wholeness and achievement in a broken culture.

These loving instructions for parents originate in God's love. Authentic biblical learning is rooted in understanding and keeping these foundational instructions. We will explore these instructions in detail in Chapters 5-8.

CHAPTER 5

# Pathways of Life

## God's Loving Instructions

As explained in the previous chapter, the starting point for an authentic biblical education is established by God's Magna Charta for home-based biblical teaching given to parents in Deuteronomy 6:1-9. As the primary tutors for their children in their own homes, parents are summoned to know and experience the fear of God and embrace the wholehearted keeping of His commandments first in their hearts and lifestyles. This is accomplished through the grace of God and the presence of the Holy Spirit in the lives of the parents. As a result, parents become living examples as well as instructors for their children.

The curriculum, which is not only taught but, more importantly, *caught* in this daily process is the very nature and commandments of God. Parents who honestly walk in a loving relationship with God and obedience to His commandments impart much more than academic knowledge. They impart the legacy of their hearts to their children. The rewards are immense.

In any building project, deep and accurately designed foundations determine the strength, beauty, and usefulness of the structure. Though usually hidden beneath the earth, these foundations support the entire construction visible above the ground. Likewise, the rooting of God's loving instructions in the soil of children's hearts become the foundation for the visible and real expressions of conduct, learning, and achievement for them throughout life.

It bears repeating that the preamble to God's loving instructions (commandments) was based wholly and solely on God's caring nature and His loving actions[69] for His people, not on any merit of the people themselves. "The LORD did not choose you and lavish his love on you because you were larger or greater than other nations, for you were the smallest of all nations! It was simply because the LORD loves you, and because he was keeping the oath he had sworn to your ancestors. That is why the LORD rescued you with such amazing power from your slavery under Pharaoh in Egypt. Understand, therefore, that the LORD your God is indeed God. He is the faithful God who keeps his covenant for a thousand generations and constantly loves those who love him and obey his commands."[70] This whole communication reveals the personal nature and intimate relationship that God initiated with His people. To these special people, He was *I,* not *it.* And they were *you,* not *them.*

The love of God has been expressed for all of mankind. He laid down His life, personally and intimately, in His loving act of saving everyone from the bondage of self-centered living and rebellion toward Him. Like Israel in Egypt, there was no way of personal escape from such bondage and certainly no merit to warrant such a loving act of kindness by God to bring complete deliverance. Nevertheless, after the death of Jesus, one of his closest friends

---

69 Exod. 20:2. "I am the LORD your God, who rescued you from slavery in Egypt." Their rescue was based totally on God's love, power, and intervention. Israel was utterly helpless to escape in their present position as slaves making bricks in Egypt under Pharaoh's rule.

70 Deut 7:7-9. (NLT)

wrote of him, "This is real love. It is not that we loved God, but that he loved us and sent his Son as a sacrifice to take away our sins."[71]

God's ten loving instructions are then given personally to those who already have an intimate relationship with God—given to them as a gift based entirely on His undeserved goodness. The motivation for keeping God's loving instructions spring from an awareness of God's love and best intentions for His children: so *"you will enjoy a long life and so that all will go well with you."*[72] Our keeping of God's ten loving words of instruction for us flows out of our celebration of God's grace.

We embrace God's loving instructions with genuine gratitude knowing that they have been given to us as pathways of life for our good and the good of our children.[73] The purpose of these instructions is simple and clear. A natural father commands his young child not to cross the street without looking in both directions, not because he desires to deprive his child of the experience of crossing the road but to prevent his child from being hit by a car. The father gives his command because he has an awareness much higher than that of his child. His command is motivated by his deep love and desire to care for his child.

In the very same manner, it is because there is a relationship that has already been established with God that He gives commandments to His children—to preserve life, enhance the quality of life, and assure an enduring relationship with Him.

Man, acting independently of God, is inherently self-centered and rebellious. As Harold Kushner has so aptly stated in his book, *To Life*, "It is God's concern for us that invests our every act with significance. Without the God-dimension, the issue of how people treat each other would be a matter of good manners rather than

---

[71] I Jn 4:10 (NLT).

[72] Deut. 6:2-3.

[73] Deut. 6:24.

morality. Without faith that God underwrites our understanding of right and wrong, the idea that the world belongs to the strongest and the most ruthless would be as valid a rule to live by as 'love your neighbor as yourself.'"[74]

Gradually, however, in this moral void, the pendulum for private and public decency has begun to swing back. There is a gut recognition in our national consciousness that something is amiss, that there is something seriously awry with the results of our public educational systems. Secular attempts to stem this malicious tide of moral breakdown are being made. Law schools have reinstituted courses on ethics. The military has made ethics a significant focus of study in their institutional curriculum, and public schools have added classes in "values education" in which students are encouraged to embrace positive values on rational grounds.

Unfortunately, the success of such programs is limited for reasons that are rooted in the structure of the Ten Commandments themselves. Significantly, the first four commandments teach *love for God*, and the last six commandments teach *love and respect for others*. The problem is that these programs attempt to enact the ethics of the second half of the commandments, which have to do with *loving others*. These principles cannot be effectively carried out before giving careful attention to the first half of the commandments, which emphasize *loving God*. It is out of genuine love for God that man can authentically love others, and therefore to keep the ethics of the Ten Commandments.

Commandments 1-4 give us practical instruction on how to acquire reverence for God and commandments 5-10 teach us how to show respect for others. Revering God becomes the life source out of which springs love and respect for others. Authentic love for God and genuine respect for others offers the anecdote to the

[74] Harold S. Kushner, *To Life!: A Celebration of Jewish Being and Thinking* (New York: Warner Books, 1993), 144.

malignancy of our present moral corruption. Loving God and loving our neighbor is the root of authentic biblical learning.

It is time to examine these pathways of life carefully. Each of God's loving commandments is expressed in the second person singular. Each of the Ten Commandments is given with a personal and individual appeal...***You*** shall. Hence each loving instruction must be kept *individually*. Each one of these words is based on God's grace, and each one has been given by a loving God who gives them to His children as a gift of His grace. The motivation for the keeping of all of God's commandments is love for God. Blessing follows the keeping of these words. Each commandment is a priceless gift to be kept and cherished.

## CHAPTER 6

# Yahweh's Ten Loving Instructions

## Loving God – His First Three Words

### *ONE*

*Interestingly,* the first commandment addresses the very core of human existence, the invisible inner personality, or the heart of man. But then, why shouldn't it?

"***You***...do not worship any other gods besides me."[75]

All individuals devote themselves to some object of internal or external affection more than to any other. All of life is worship. Whatever we make the center of our lives determines whether we are devoted to the worship of the true God or a false one. The meaning of "do not worship any god besides me" is unequivocal: *Nothing* is to take the place of the true God.

There is to be nothing in existence within our heart that displaces the priority of loving God with all of ones' being—no ideology, pleasure, possession, or person, whether real or imaginary. Ultimately, the commandments that a person keeps (or does not keep) show which God that person is serving.

It's not difficult to identify some of the "first-placed" false gods of our day. We will look at a few. You probably can think of more.

---

[75] Exod. 20:3.

As you reflect on the false gods listed below, the question we all must answer is: Are there any false gods in *my* heart?

### *Ideology or Philosophy*

Man's self-absorption has led to the widespread belief that each man is his own god. With his superior mental prowess (in his inflated mind), he believes his inner thoughts hold the answers to all of life's mysteries. Whatever he thinks, he believes is true. Out of this mindset evolve countless ideologies and philosophies that deny the supremacy of the one true God.

Humanism runs rampant in our culture. Even Christians can fall prey to this cunning ideology by relying on their logic in making decisions or solving problems rather than surrendering to the all-knowing God in prayer.

Many philosophies disguise themselves as truth. For example, statements like "everything happens for a reason" and "it will all work out the way it's supposed to" fall short when we compare them to the full scope of Scripture. Important elements such as surrender and obedience are missing from such empty philosophies.

Public opinion polls have become the new basis for instituting public policy. Darwin's theory of evolution has impacted the practice of law and public policy, severing a connection with moral standards. The Supreme Court relies heavily on definitions in dictionaries (as many as five different ones) to determine legal rulings. Accepted norms for centuries are being changed.[76] Dictionaries

[76] Noah Webster (1828), a lawyer by training, often called *the Father of American Scholarship and Education* defines *marriage* as a specifically heterosexual union. He further defines marriage as "The act of uniting a man and woman for life; wedlock; the legal union of a man and woman for life. Marriage is a contract both civil and religious, by which the parties engage to live together in mutual affection and fidelity, till death shall separate them. Marriage was instituted by God himself for the purpose of preventing the promiscuous intercourse of the sexes, for promoting domestic felicity, and

have modified their commonly accepted definition of *marriage* as social attitudes toward marriage have changed. Since people's opinions are always in flux, so too, clear standards of morality have become obscured and changed.

Technology has also become one of man's chief gods. It's as if the god of technology offers *magical* hope. Man's ingenuity and technological wizardry are thought to hold the potential for solving most, if not all, of man's most significant health, environmental, and even social needs.

Ironically, this great but false god carries its inherent nemesis. At the turn of this century, the Y2K computer problem purportedly was going to turn all communication, banking, transportation, and distribution systems into utter chaos, potentially creating unparalleled catastrophes. That never happened. One would think that upon recognizing the apparent oversight and design failure *on man's part* in allowing the inherent nemesis of the 2000 computer bug, that our "high tech" society would adopt a more sobering view of the limitations and failings of this god. Still, technology continues to be exalted as the source of ultimate solutions for almost all of man's ills.

Educational theories often disguise themselves as false gods as well. Any idea or educational approach that either blatantly or subtlety displaces the primacy of God is none other than a false god.

---

for securing the maintenance and education of children". In 2003, *Merriam-Webster's Collegiate Dictionary,* an authority frequently cited by the courts, added same-sex unions to its definition of *marriage:* "1a (1) the state of being united to a person of the opposite sex as husband or wife in a consensual and contractual relationship recognized by law (2): the state of being united to a person of the same sex in a relationship like that of a traditional marriage". The *Oxford English Dictionary,* another favorite with judges, has also added same-sex marriage to its definition: "persons married to each other; matrimony. The term is now sometimes used with reference to long-term relationships between partners of the same sex". And in 2011, the *American Heritage Dictionary* added both same-sex marriage and polygamy to its definition of *marriage.*

Education reformers and politicians with lofty campaign promises have long contributed to the narrative that education can do it all. Many attempts at education reform, particularly those reforms aimed at changing some larger social problem, don't work. How many educational reforms have been proposed to eradicate poverty? Has it worked?

Any of man's philosophies or ideologies that promote themselves above the first place of God Himself in the hearts of men qualify as false gods.

### *Pleasure*

Man's appetites, sex, entertainment, and the pursuit of the ultimate recreational sport have become all-consuming passions. Just a few minutes of watching television commercials quickly reveal the images of modern cultures' gods.

Primetime devotes part of its program "menu" to the creation of culinary delights. Eating has become a national pastime and it is something I enjoy greatly. But living to eat, rather than eating to live, can lead to a deceitful passion for food, causing obesity and premature death.

Physical fitness is worthwhile. But on the flip side of becoming a servant to one's appetite, the pursuit of the perfect body, male or female, may become an all-consuming passion. The lyrics in one of Bob Dylan's songs, say it all, "you're gonna have to serve somebody."

Hollywood for years has produced new box office records. Theater temples have welcomed faithful weekend worshipers who wait in line to gain access to pay homage to the latest stars of cinema. COVID-19 simply pushed this industry more deeply into home theater venues with the latest streaming devices and services.

Others devote every waking moment in a quest to become an extreme sports star. If successful, these heroes and heroines will be rewarded with substantial financial offers for their endorsements of unique products and happily receive the worship of their proselytes who aspire to be like them. Those athletes failing to place within the ranks of the elite will quickly be discarded and forgotten as ordinary people, while the remaining mighty command millions of dollars of new contracts to go on performing their incredible acts. There are not enough seats for those who will pay any price to participate in the adoration of their sport's heroes.

Such pleasures have captivated many and have become the all-consuming focus and motivation for living. Each of these pleasures in and of themselves, when decently ordered in a person's life, are a joyful part of living. But when any pleasure becomes a person's primary focus, it becomes a misplaced priority and holds the potential for becoming a person's god.

### *Possession*

We are living in an uncertain world where natural disasters are claiming lives. We are being told a global warming trend may melt polar ice, thereby causing the oceans to rise, subsequently flooding coastal areas. Amid such uncertainties, surely a man can trust in his car, find security in his insurance policy (even though he may lose his job tomorrow and be unable to pay for it), and find peace of mind in his deodorant. Sadly, man pursues the means to accumulate these things as if the commercials were true.

A flourishing economy can also be a powerful distraction. It is in this god (a good economy) we trust. No cost seems too high to pay, including the willing dismissal and breaking of laws, as long as there are no threats to our pocketbooks. Money has become a god and the economy must be protected at any price.

The accumulation of possessions has overrun the ability to live within a balanced budget for many. Misuse of credit can subtly force folks into debtors' prison. "The rich rules over the poor, And the borrower *becomes* the lender's slave" (Prov. 22:7).

The false god of materialism subtly offers the *elusive hope* that there must be some financial solution for our issues.

### *Person*

A sports hero, celebrity, marriage partner, or any person who becomes wrongly misplaced in our priorities can become our god. Do the amount of time, expense, and devotion to a person within any of these categories surpass the same expression and expenditure of time and resources to the one true and living God, who is *first of all* deserving of our wholehearted love?

Perhaps the worship of *man himself* has become the most insidious and incestuous form of worship of a false god today. A glance at the progression of magazine titles over the last few decades reveals this shift in focus.

In the 1950s, *Life* magazine conveyed there was more to life than the man himself. With some sense of the wonder of the universe, earth, and man's place in God's scheme of creation, the magazine *Life* reflected the multifaceted wonder from man's perspective of all creation and his unusual place in it. A man was a small but significant person in a created universe who drew his meaning for existence in relationship to a magnificent loving creator.

A few years later in the early '70s, a red and black *Time* magazine cover declared "God is Dead." That was during the tumultuous days of rioting and torching of inner cities and Vietnam. Since for many, God did die in their minds and hearts as they succumbed to the false ideologies of relativism and secularism, man became the center of his own universe. "If it feels good, do it."

Unfortunately, with every person becoming the center and standard for doing only those things that felt good to themselves, other unsuspecting people are injured, albeit perhaps unintentionally, as with the kingdom of the god of relativism and Aids. What feels good for someone may ultimately result in the death of another.

Subsequently, with God gone from the scene, the publication of *People* magazine gained full and widespread acceptance with its new focus on people, i.e., the rich and the famous. Still, there was a recognition of many people in the community, people in relationships with others. Then the magazine *Self* appeared as the new anchor to the public newsstand. Today the most common and exalted god-given priority over God is *self.* "Techno man" has replaced God as the center of his universe. And it is becoming a moral black hole.

Self rules! Selfies! Put yourself first in all things. *Self* consummated the marriage of materialism and relativism. Image matters more than substance.

But the god of self is a whimsical god disconnected from the nature of a loving God and His loving instructions. With a man at the center, and relativism as one's guide, what is right today may be wrong tomorrow. Public opinion polls are often swayed by the loudest voices and the media.

Unfortunately, man's rebellious spirit and unlawful behavior assure him of his destruction apart from the intervention that comes out of a relationship to the one true God.

To be clear, no ideology, pleasure, possession, or person, whether it is real or imaginary, is in and of itself a false god. It is in giving any one of these a preeminence that displaces the primacy of the true God in our heart that results in worship of a false god. *Nothing* is to replace God from occupying *first place* in the heart of man. Because God deeply loves man, this prohibition against the existence of any false god in a person's life is for the individual's welfare. To allow a false god to take up rule in one's life deprives one of receiving God's best.

Beyond the negative side of not following this first commandment, there is an astonishing positive side *when we do follow it*: If we let Him, God will give us Himself. He wants to! The positive side of "you shall have no other gods before me" is found in Israel's Shema, "you shall love Jehovah your God with all your heart, and with all your soul, and with all your strength."[77] In other words, you shall *have Me*, and you shall *love Me*! Jesus, when asked by the religious rulers of His day to give them the greatest commandment, replied, "Love the Lord your God with all your heart and with all your soul and with all your mind. This is the first and greatest commandment."[78]

As I mentioned earlier, Solomon's warning to his learners was to make the keeping of their heart the number one priority in all of life because the heart is the wellspring of everyone's entire being and core of personality. To be in love with God transforms all that we are and affects all we do. What could be more important than that?

This truth is the foundation of all authentic, wholehearted learning. Wholehearted learning is a relational education based on knowing God and experiencing God's love.[79] Such a relation-

---

[77] Deut. 6:5.

[78] Matt. 22:37-38.

[79] The earliest account of Harvard which appeared in London in 1643 was taken from *New England's First Fruits,* published by Samuel Eliot Morrison. This document among other things, cited the rules and precepts of Harvard: "Let every student be plainly instructed and earnestly pressed to consider well the main end of his life and studies is to know God and Jesus Christ which is eternal life, John 17:3 and therefore to lay Christ in the bottom, as the only foundation of all sound knowledge and learning." The founders of Harvard were, or course, the Puritans. Far from being reactionary, dogmatic, judgmental, intolerant primitives that modern students often imagine, these were an enlightened people who wished to cast off the darkness of Europe's

ship opens the door to a new and fulfilled quality of life, positive transformation of character, and a reformed lifestyle.

Our children will recognize the chief objects of our affection and devotion. They are profoundly great imitators being inescapably touched by those they are close to. Will they see by our example that loving God is our number one priority?

## *TWO*

At first glance, the second commandment might appear to simply be a duplication of the first,

"***You***...do not make idols of any kind, whether in the shape of birds or animals or fish. You must never worship or bow down to them, for I, the LORD your God, am a jealous God who will not share your affection with any other god! I do not leave unpunished the sins of those who hate me, but I punish the children for

---

feudal past and forge a new type of society. Samuel Eliot Morrison, foremost Harvard historian, describes their ideology as follows: "The Puritan creed... stimulated mental activity on the part of those who professed it," with the ministers maintaining "Open-minded and receptive attitudes toward scientific discoveries." The Puritan religion provided the "dynamic motive for the intellectual movement in New England..." Far from being ethereal mystics, the Puritans believed that Truth, in part was knowable through the five senses, and through empirical research and reasoning. But the idea that all Truth was knowable could only be fathomed in the realm of Faith, they argued. Visitors to Harvard need only to view the Harvard seal on one of the gates to see this illustrated. A stone rendering of the Harvard seal portrays three books; two are set faced up, while the third is displayed face down. A people who viewed all symbols as having great meaning no doubt meant this third book to signify the Truth that was hidden from reason. This was the Truth that could come only through divine revelation and Faith. Before we dismiss the Harvard founders as being crude and unsophisticated, we should remember that it was their form of civil government, although not perfected, which became the working model for the world's first successful democracy. This form of government is being imitated all over the world in our day. Excerpt taken from "The Forerunner International," Vol. 1, No. 1 (Fall 1997).

the sins of their parents to the third and fourth generations. But I lavish my love on those who love me and obey my commands, even for a thousand generations."[80]

The first commandment forbids the existence of other gods, while the second commandment forbids the creating, producing, or making of other gods—idols. The first can be broken *unconsciously,* while the second involves the volitional making of an idol or *conscious* breaking of God's command.

Addressed in this second command is God's prohibition against a man making either real or mental figures, objects, or images representative of a god as aids to worship.[81] Because God is so extraordinarily greater than man, this prohibition focuses on God's protection of man's inherent propensity to create God in man's image. This, too, is for man's good.

Listen to God's word in Deuteronomy 4:15-20, "But be careful! You did not see the LORD's form on the day he spoke to you from the fire at Mount Sinai. So do not corrupt yourselves by making a visible image in any form—whether of a man or a woman, an animal or a bird, a creeping creature, or a fish. And when you look up into the sky and see the sun, moon, and stars—all the forces of heaven—do not be seduced by them and worship them. The LORD, your God, designated these heavenly bodies for all the peoples of the earth. Remember that the LORD rescued you from the burning furnace of Egypt to become his people and special possession; that is what you are today."

There are penetrating reasons for us not to make man-made images of the God who revealed himself at Mt. Sinai. God is

---

80 Exod. 20:4-6. (NLT)

81 Obviously, this does not forbid the sculpturing and painting of images of living things. God himself directed that cherubim be sculpted to preside over the Ark of the Covenant and also be woven into the veil of the Holy of Holies, as well as commanding the embroidery of lilies and pomegranates. Solomon's Temple displayed lions, bulls, and cherubim. (cf. 1 Kings 7:18-20).

limitless. He cannot be confined in marble or paint! To limit God, in a sense, then is to deny Him. Such images obscure God's glory, as well.

"The problem with images of God is that while they are ostensibly made to reveal aspects of God, they end up hiding the real God. For example, when Aaron made the golden calf (the bull image), he thought he was honoring God by using such a symbol of power—'Here is the bull who charged before you to bring you out of Egypt.' But Aaron was unwittingly masking and degrading God, for how could a bull reveal God's moral excellence, goodness, and loving grace? It may well be that the orgy that ignited in front of the golden bull image happened because the bull was not only a symbol of strength but of virility and sexual power. *Our human tendency is to become like the gods we worship.*"[82]

Further, when we imagine that God is represented in a statue or painting, we begin to believe He is subtly localized. For example, many paintings have depicted Jesus as a white Anglo- Saxon. But Jesus (Yeshua) was a Jew. It is important to know Him for who He is. Isaiah 53:2 in the Complete Jewish Bible reads, "He was not well-formed or especially handsome; we saw him, but his appearance did not attract us." Yeshua was not attractive or impressive in the flesh. When you think about it, this makes obvious sense. God could not send an attractive man. He needed us to be attracted by the character, deeds, and power of Yeshua—by the truth. Our culture, world, and churches are rife with false ideas and misrepresentations of who God is (as well as religious traditions) without any valid biblical basis. God cannot be confined. Although man

---

[82] R.Kent Hughes, Disciplines of Grace (Wheaton: Crossway Books, 1993), pp. 46-47.

has been created in God's image,[83] God is separate and higher than man.[84]

By creating images of God, a man also projects his weaknesses back onto Him. With this command, God desires to spare us from placing our imperfections on an image that might dimmish who He is apart from us.

Additionally, through such images, a person attempts to "control" and "own" God to run their universe, to maximize their need fulfillment. To do so is always attractive and comfortable for the corrupt heart. But the God of the universe cannot be imprisoned in the images that are constructed by men.

Finally, the tragic consequence of the worship of a created image of God is that idols subtract from all we have genuinely received from God Himself. Idols subvert the revelation we have of God through nature, conscience, Scripture, and by His own Son.[85] In sum, images of God limit, obscure, localize, project, control, and subtract from an awesome and loving God who must reveal Himself to us for us to honestly and accurately know Him as He is.

But this commandment is far more profound than most of us have understood. Not only does this commandment forbid making material images of God. It prohibits our creating mental images as well. To construct mental idols is also a massive breach of the second commandment. The making of our mental images subtly breaks this command by defining on our own who we think— or would like to think— God is. We tend to grab hold of those

---

83 Gen. 1:26.

84 "My thoughts are completely different from yours," says the LORD. "And my ways are far beyond anything you could imagine. For just as the heavens are higher than the earth, so are my ways higher than your ways and my thoughts higher than your thoughts." Isa 55:8-9. (NLT)

85 "Long ago God spoke many times and in many ways to our ancestors through the prophets. But now in these final days, he has spoken to us through his Son." Heb 1:1-2 (NLT)

aspects of God that appeal to us while denying something else that the Scriptures teach about God.

For example, we may embrace every word that shows us that God is forgiving and merciful while rejecting the descriptions of God as a judge and a consuming fire. To simply muse subjectively about God's being is both inadequate and misleading. We must embrace both the things we like to think about God and the things we do not wish to think about Him. To do so requires constant humility and a willingness to change. Our ideas or mental images of God must continually give way to the real and living God who reveals himself through His word and His Son.

God's gracious goal for giving man this second commandment is to bring man into a living relationship with the real, personal, and living God rather than man's fabricated or imagined mental images of who he thinks God is. Seeing God accurately destroys our false mental images, breaks the power of faulty religious traditions that have become subtle idols in our lives, and introduces beautiful new freedom to love Him more fully. I have learned that the more clearly I see God for who He is, the more my heart becomes enlarged to love Him.

## *THREE*

The third loving instruction for us is, "***You***...do not misuse the name of the LORD your God. The LORD will not let you go unpunished if you misuse his name."[86]

Name, as it is used in this commandment, is not a mere designation but a description of the character, in this case, that of Yahweh,[87] your God. It is the redemptive name of the God who

---

[86] Exod. 20:7.

[87] Please see footnote 61, chapter 4. God's name Yahweh reveals His character and nature.

chose His people and delivered them from bondage. It is the covenantal name of God, who keeps His promises to His people. And it is the relational name of the God who establishes a relationship out of His concern for man, granting His faithful presence to those who trust Him.

"This name was held so sacred that it was pronounced only once a year by the priest when giving the blessing on the great Day of Atonement (Leviticus 23:27). Israel came to value the name so much that when scribes copied the manuscripts and came to the name Yahweh, they would stop, ceremonially bathe all over, and then go back to the scroll with an unused pen. Yahweh is the awesome, personal, covenantal name of God that must not be misused."[88] Yahweh is a precious and awesome name.

To misuse the name of the LORD is to carry (take) His name falsely with worthless or insincere behavior. It is to use the name of your God, who is entirely faithful and promise-keeping, in an empty way. In the Old Testament, the primary misuse of God's name was the result of breaking an oath.[89]

Today's counterpart of such an oath is the simple keeping of a promise. In our society and culture, verbal contracts are no longer considered legal or binding. Hence the voluminous requirements we all experience in establishing written documents to substantiate all contractual agreements between parties. But as believers, because we bear His precious name, whether we have verbalized it or not, any promise we make is made in the presence of God and must be kept whether or not it has been written down. Any relationship in which our words and the keeping of any promise are not radically sincere and truthful misuses the name of the Lord our God.

---

88 Hughes, p. 55.

89 See Leviticus 19:12, Numbers 30:2, and Deuteronomy 23:21-23.

Rudeness and crudeness characterize our culture of today. Vulgarity has been confused with honesty. Language has become irreverent both to God and man. The name of God is degraded, abused, and blasphemed. Those who engage in such misuse of God's name are now considered by others in our culture as amusing and "with it."

When asked to teach His disciples how to pray, Jesus first taught them the importance of honoring His Father's name.[90] In contrast to the reverence that Jesus Himself taught his followers for the name of His heavenly Father, Bart Simpsons' "grace" is a true reflection of our society's stance in defaming the precious name and nature of God: "We made all this stuff. So, thanks for nothing! Amen." Such corrupt verbal utterance reveals irreverence and contempt toward Yahweh, which is a blatant abuse of God's name.

Cursing others, or damning someone in God's name, is the ultimate depth in misusing God's name. How we verbally address or reference another person has a profound effect on our regard and treatment of that individual. All forms of speech, whether the breaking of a promise, irreverence, blatant contempt, or using God's name to curse another person all are a misuse of the precious name of the LORD. The abuse of God's name and growth in our love of God are mutually exclusive. The more intimate our relationship is with God, the more accurately we will perceive Him for who He is, and the more we will love Him. The more abundant our own experience of knowing God's love for us personally, the

---

[90] "Pray like this: Our Father in heaven, may your name be honored." (Matthew 6:9). As those who follow Christ, to "hallow the name" (honor) includes not only the inward attitude and outward action of profound reverence and active praise, but also that personal godliness, loving obedience and aggressive Christlikeness, which reveal the presence of God in the life, which is His true earthly glory. (from International Standard Bible Encylopaedia, Electronic Database Copyright (C) 1996 http://www.Biblesoft.com)

less will be our tendency to curse others. As we honor and reverence the name of the LORD in our thoughts and prayers, our communication of real love and esteem to our family members and those we encounter daily will become a divine verbal path to loving God more fully.

In this process of renewal for ourselves, we will nourish our spouse and children with the love of God Himself. God's love that is expressed through us as parents to one another and our children becomes the "miracle grow" for the emotional, spiritual, and intellectual development and well-being of our children. Through our attitudes and spoken words to our family members, and to all those we come in contact with, we reflect and can impart sincere and holy respect for the name of Yahweh to our children. Our speech patterns and attitudes will become a foundation for nurturing and protecting them their entire lives as they receive deep respect to honor the name of the LORD as they observe and experience our intimate verbal behavior with them, our friends, acquaintances, and even our enemies.

## CHAPTER 7

# Yahweh's Ten Loving Instructions

## Loving God – His Fourth Word

### *FOUR*

***Rest!*** Among God's loving instructions, I have discovered this precious word to be an absolute gem. God's fourth word to us is,

"**You**...Remember to observe the Sabbath day by keeping it holy. Six days a week are set apart for your daily duties and regular work, but the seventh day is a day of rest dedicated to the LORD your God. On that day, no one in your household may do any work. This includes you, your sons and daughters, your male and female servants, your livestock, and any foreigners living among you. For in six days, the LORD made the heavens, the earth, the sea, and everything in them; then he rested on the seventh day. That is why the LORD blessed the Sabbath day and set it apart as holy."[91]

Because of the importance of this commandment, it is treated more extensively than any of the other commandments.

Some years ago, while we were living in northern Wisconsin, I was touched deeply by this precious word from God. That experience forever altered my perception and understanding of this gracious, loving instruction regarding rest from our heavenly Father.

---

[91] Exod. 20:8-11. (NLT)

This life-changing event occurred to me one Saturday morning in early summer. I had taken one of our chairs outside and propped it up against our mobile home to spend some time reading God's word. On a small point of land surrounded by water in the pristine rolling hills of Wisconsin's farm country, it was not unusual to hear the mating calls of deer just behind our trailer at night. In the spring, I would awake to a beautiful thanksgiving chorus of a multitude of songbirds. During the summer, Marengo Lake was God's swimming hole for us, and with a boat and fishing pole, it was also a generous source of crappie, perch, bluegill, and northern pike.

Since our trailer was pink, and we were surrounded by water, it was only appropriate that we affectionately named our trailer the Pink Flamingo. It came equipped with an oil furnace and Ashley wood burning stove. The walls of the Pink Flamingo were thin, so we quickly felt changes in outdoor temperatures inside our little home. Sometimes, during the Siberian cold of winter, our pillowcases would freeze to the wood paneling in the back bedroom. We had to pull them free when we awoke in the morning.

It was here that we welcomed our first son into our family. Gretchen gave birth to Andrew at Bayfield Hospital on December 24th. A couple of days later, we brought the first of God's three beautiful children back to the Pink Flamingo in the dead of winter.

That summer morning, I flipped open my Bible and began reading. It just so happened that I was reading the Creation account.[92] As I read this account, I understood for the first time—with my heart—the purpose of the Sabbath.

First and foremost, I realized the Sabbath was God's gift of physical rest for me. My heart melted as I understood that God, as my loving Father, cared enough about me to set aside a day for my rest, relaxation, and refreshing. He knew that after six days of labor, I needed a break.

---

92 Gen. 1-2. See especially Gen. 2:1-3.

Since God created man, He understands that we need to renew our physical beings. Stress is one of the most debilitating maladies of our time. God has supplied a provision and remedy for man's exhaustion since the beginning of time. He placed a mini-vacation at the end of every week for all of humanity.

Although I had belonged to God for years, on a summer day in Wisconsin the Holy Spirit revealed our Father's instructions regarding rest to me *personally*. That morning I experienced the presence of our loving heavenly Father freshly and vibrantly. God Himself wrote this law of rest into my heart and transformed my thinking. He gave me an entirely new perspective about the purpose of the Sabbath day and His gift of rest to me. The presence and work of the Holy Spirit had liberated me from my religious misconceptions about Sunday and Sabbath that I had believed my entire life.

The replacement of Sunday from the biblical Sabbath has been a tradition in the Catholic and Protestant churches for nearly 2000 years. Documented history sheds light on how the fourth commandment was changed. On March 7, 321 A.D., the Roman Emperor Constantine I issued a civil decree making Sunday a day of rest from labor, stating: "All judges and city people and the craftsmen shall rest upon the venerable day of the sun." Hence the name *Sun*day! This religious change was the means Constantine used to expand his political empire to bring Gentiles with pagan practices under his rule. Many were sun worshippers. After Constantine made the legal decree about the change of the Sabbath to Sunday, the Catholic Church confirmed his act in one church council after another. "The church after changing the day of rest from the Jewish Sabbath or seventh day of the week to the first, made the third commandment refer to Sunday as the day to be kept holy as the Lord's day."[93] The Catholic church altered the

[93] Herbermann, Charles George, *The Catholic Encyclopedia*, Vol. 4, p. 153.

Scriptures to make this change. Malachi 3:6 says, "For I, the LORD, do not change."

Not only is Sabbath intended as God's gift of rest for the physical well-being of his children, but this is an extraordinary day that God Himself has blessed. In Hebrew, s*abat* (or *Sabbath*) has one central meaning: cessation of activity.[94] This word first is used in Genesis 2:2. "On the seventh day, having finished his task, God *rested* from all his work." In addition to resting on the seventh day, God did two additional things regarding this day. The next verse says, "And God blessed the seventh day and declared it holy because it was the day when he rested from his work of creation." Thus God not only rested on the seventh day, but He *blessed* it and *sanctified* (declared it holy) it, which means He set it apart as a day unique, special, and different from the other six days of the week.

The sanctification of this particular day confers the same concept of Holiness at a specific *time* just as God summons His people into the *state* of Holiness.[95] Harris, Archer Jr., and Waltke write, "Everything God made, as recorded in Genesis, he called good. Only the Sabbath, however, he sanctified, indicating perhaps that the climax of creation was not the creation of man, as is often stated, but the day of rest, the seventh day. The Sabbath is thus an invitation to rejoice in God's creation and recognize God's sovereignty over our time."[96]

---

[94] Harris, Archer, Jr., Waltke, *Theological Wordbook of the Old Testament*, p. 902. "The basic thrust of the verb is, when transitive, "to sever, put an end to," and when intransitive, "to desist, to come to an end." This may possibly indicate that the Sabbath is the day which 'puts a stop to' the week's work."

[95] 1 Pet 2:9 says, "But you are not like that, for you are a chosen people. You are a kingdom of priests, God's *holy nation*, his very own possession. This is so you can show others the goodness of God, for he called you out of the darkness into his wonderful light." (NLT) Please see footnote 22, in Chapter 2, for an explanation of true Biblical holiness.

[96] Harris, Archer, Jr., Waltke, *Theological Wordbook of the Old Testament*, p. 903.

In practical terms, the Sabbath is separated (or sanctified from the other days of the week) by establishing an actual boundary between this one day of the week with the other six. Sabbath rest comes as the result of making a complete break with the everyday toils and concerns we have devoted our energy to all week long. Empty your pockets so you carry nothing into the Sabbath and focus your conversation on uplifting things, rather than everyday problems and those things that are happening in the world today.

Besides taking a break from ordinary everyday activities (which yields real physical rest), when we choose to dedicate the day to noble use we discover the blessing God has given to this day. It is much more than a flight from the world. It is an *entry* into a period of exceptional and pleasing enjoyment.

Isaiah 58:13 calls Sabbath a *delight*. As we honor Him, God recognizes our genuine desire for His friendship. Extending such a welcome to our maker is an invitation He will never turn down. His vibrant presence becomes a sweet reward. Just as God enjoyed fellowship in the garden of Eden with Adam and Eve, He desires to sit down with us and enjoy our company. The outcome is a *holy rest*.

For those of us who are tyrants of time, who are in relentless pursuit of material gain, it is difficult to grasp the fact that God's first blessing did not focus on material prosperity or the acquisition of wealth or goods. Instead, God's blessing was placed first *on time*!

In his excellent book, *To Life,* Harold S. Kushner writes, "The holy days of the Jewish calendar have been called 'cathedrals in time.'...We control time: time does not control us. … If the Israelites should have learned one thing from their Egyptian experience, it is that God wants human beings to be free, to serve Him, and not a human master. Claiming your right to rest on the Sabbath is a way of living out that idea. … The two words used in biblical Hebrew to describe God resting on that first Sabbath are not the usual words for resting. The first word means 'He ceased His labors,' and the second word means 'He got His soul back.' We are commanded to rest on the seventh day first to demonstrate our freedom from slavery, and second to get our souls back."[97]

Kushner sums up his perspective on the Sabbath by saying, "And finally, Sabbath rest is a time of detaching ourselves for a day from all of our problems, everything unpleasant and unfinished. Resting one day makes you a better worker on the other six. But I would like to think that Sabbath observance, like virtue, is its reward, that it is worth doing not because it makes you a better worker, but because it makes you a better human being in those parts of your life that have nothing to do with work."[98]

Entering a *real* rest for one entire day (sunset Friday to sunset Saturday) of the week is not natural. Our God is so practical. He knows how easy it is for us to forget. That is why He says, "*Remember* the Sabbath day to keep it holy." (Exodus 20:8)

As you begin to try to move into this blessing of God, you will likely find that not only is everything in your constitution programmed to resist such a rest ("Oh, I just can't take this time out... I've got too much to do!"), but you will encounter resistance from the spiritual realm as well as others, perhaps even some of your closest friends. There is such a profound blessing in the proper use of this day that Satan will orchestrate his strategies in an attempt to withhold from you the rewards of rest and this weekly experience of God's presence. (Remember, he is a thief and a robber. John 10:10)

Nevertheless, the joy and delight intended for you by God himself await you as you make a conscious choice to establish and cultivate this new habit. Genuine weekly rest is a part of your inheritance as God's child. One of the main results of celebrating

---

97 Harold S. Kushner, *To Life!: A Celebration of Jewish Being and Thinking*, 92-97.

98 Ibid. 98-100.

the Sabbath is that over time, you will find yourself walking more and more as the new creation that God is forming within you and that you want to be. The joy of His special presence experienced during this day of rest will flow with you into the rest of the week. This blessing profoundly touches every area of our lives mentally and spiritually as well. I have learned over time that I want to be a full participant in anything that has the blessing of Yahweh upon it.

During the last couple of years just before Andrew and Elizabeth left home for college, we had begun to discover that entering into a genuine rest together as a family was becoming a precious time for emotional healing. Our rest time fostered an environment for restoring lost personhood that our quick flash society and fragmented world bombarded daily. At the beginning of the Friday evening meal, Gretchen would light the Shabbat candles and offer the Hebrew blessing as we entered our Sabbath rest.[99] We discovered that this radical break from the demands of all of our lives throughout the week, facilitated reestablishing honest, forgiving relationships with one another.

Our present age is one of broken promises and fractured relationships. With time to focus on our relationships, we would ask for and receive forgiveness for any unsettled failures or wrongs committed against one another during the past week. Addressing hurts repairs relationships and brings healing. It is wonderfully satisfying to have our inner lives mended and to experience healing for any misunderstandings or brokenness in our lives with one another as a family. Since we all desired the presence of God to be with us, we understood that we had to make sure our relationships with each other were first made right.

---

99 For an extensive and helpful introduction into the special ways and benefits that believing families can develop a real Sabbath observance together, see *Celebrate the Feasts* by Martha Zimmerman.

How often do families enjoy a meal together with no deadlines to meet or places to go? The delight of Shabbat invited us back into a thoroughly human dimension of living. We discovered the wholeness of relationships that were made possible, given the gift of unhurried time. It took a commitment from each of us, but the reward was an evening and a day to kick off our shoes, relax, and enjoy each other.

After supper, I gladly would place my hands on each of our children to bless them and pray for God's best for their lives. How many children today are receiving weekly encouragement and blessing from their parents? Can you imagine what security and strength are imparted to our children when they know they have the approval of their parents *and* the blessing of God working for them, especially considering the vicious world of peer pressure and compromise they encounter every day?

And in a deliberate restfulness, we welcomed the presence of God with us. God is living and creative; He wishes to make Himself known. To use a popular phrase, I learned that God had a desire to "hang out" with us too. God is not religious. He is real. As a family, we watched God express Himself differently from week to week. Along with listening for God's voice through His Spirit and Word and enjoying each other, we discovered that God's blessing on Sabbath released us into *unhurried* time to enjoy delightful adventures together. During this season of our lives, we were living in Virginia Beach near the Atlantic Ocean. We took spontaneous trips to the beach with our Golden Retriever coming along with us. Wave surfing and watching dolphins refreshed us. And then there were the after beach treats at Dairy Queen on our way home. We just allowed each other to be creative in what we might like to do. We have a wonderful heavenly Father who enjoys giving good gifts to his children.

Sabbath was not a legalistic rule that we were trying to follow, but a relationship with a living God and with one another. This special day became a time for each one of us to develop and flourish.

Because God has placed a special blessing on the Sabbath day, one of my greatest personal joys has been receiving an outpouring of God's revelation to me—without even trying! I have found that God opens His word and shows things to me that I am unable to dig out at other times when employing my best study habits and using all the biblical research tools at my disposal. God is always waiting. It is just that it is so difficult to quiet ourselves enough in real rest to hear Him speaking to us.

I believe it is in this restful Sabbath setting that God desires to come and fellowship with us just as He communed with Adam and Eve in the cool of the Garden of Eden. I wonder how many hearts and homes He is waiting to enter as we rush out to fill our lives with our pleasures and pursuits on His holy day.[100]

---

[100] See Isa. 58:1-14. Isa. 58:13-14 states, "If because of the Sabbath, you turn your foot from doing your {own} pleasure on My holy day, and call the Sabbath a delight, the holy {day} of the LORD honorable, and honor it (Him), desisting from your {own} ways, from seeking your {own} pleasure and speaking {your own} word, Then you will take delight in the LORD, and I will make you ride on the heights of the earth; and I will feed you {with} the heritage of Jacob your father, for the mouth of the LORD has spoken." (NAU) Even the secular world recognizes the value of rest but has changed the Sabbath into a weekend and substitutes sports, vacations, entertainment, drugs, and alcohol for the presence of God. Instead of life and restoration, which is the outcome of genuine Sabbath rest, man's own choice of activities often contributes to increased levels of stress, leads to exhaustion, and produces broken relationships. Records show that secular holidays and weekends are marked by the greatest amount of crime, drunkenness, lewdness, and accidental deaths. As God's people we are called to be different from the world through the "renewing of the mind" (Rom. 12:2). In this regard Paul warns us "Don't let the world around you squeeze you into its own mold." As God's children our minds are always in the process of being renewed according to *divinely revealed* thought patterns and values. Learning to truly receive and enjoy this gift of rest and to separate this day as holy is truly only accomplished through God's grace and the renewing

Sabbath is also a perpetual reminder[101] (like the wedding ring) of the betrothal of God's holy people who have a covenant relationship with Yahweh that reaches into the future. There will be a final wedding feast at the return of Messiah Jesus (Yeshua).[102] Sabbath is a weekly rehearsal for the coming millennial rule of God's kingdom, which will be the ultimate display of a promise kept in a relationship between a holy God and His holy people. At that time, God's children will enjoy uninterrupted holy rest together.[103] We experience a taste of the rest that is foreshadowed in the weekly Shabbat.

As parents, we can exercise an ongoing weekly choice between rest or stress. We have a choice to enjoy a refreshing renewal as

---

of our minds. Like all of God's dealings in our lives, it is a process bathed in His grace.

[101] "So the sons of Israel shall observe the Sabbath, to celebrate the Sabbath throughout their generations as a perpetual covenant. It is a sign between Me and the sons of Israel forever; for in six days the LORD made heaven and earth, but on the seventh day He ceased {from labor,} and was refreshed." Exod. 31:16-17. (NAS)

[102] Rev. 19:9.

[103] Then I saw a new heaven and a new earth, for the old heaven and the old earth had disappeared. And the sea was also gone. And I saw the holy city, the new Jerusalem, coming down from God out of heaven like a beautiful bride prepared for her husband. I heard a loud shout from the throne, saying, "Look, the home of God is now among his people! He will live with them, and they will be his people. God himself will be with them. He will remove all of their sorrows, and there will be no more death or sorrow or crying or pain. For the old world and its evils are gone forever." And the one sitting on the throne said, "Look, I am making all things new!" And then he said to me, "Write this down, for what I tell you is trustworthy and true." And he also said, "It is finished! I am the Alpha and the Omega—the Beginning and the End. To all who are thirsty I will give the springs of the water of life without charge! All who are victorious will inherit all these blessings, and I will be their God, and they will be my children." Rev 21:1-7 (NLT) And John writes in Rev. 22:14, "Blessed are those who do His commandments, that they may have the right to the tree of life, and may enter through the gates into the city." (NKJ)

free men and women or to succumb to the unrelenting tasks and responsibilities that require our attention throughout the week. It is a profound privilege as parents to impart the inheritance of *rest* to our children.

The weekly gift of rest is a treasure from the storehouse of blessing found in the wonderful loving instruction in God's fourth commandment. It is one of the expressions of care for us from our heavenly Father who deeply loves us, blesses us abundantly, and gives us the gift of weekly rest.

The first four commandments help provide a road map for us to understand how to build our relationship with a God who deeply loves us. By learning to make our love for Him our priority, by removing all material and mental idols and filling our lives with Him, honoring His name, and by keeping an ongoing sanctuary of time for the restoration of ourselves and the delight of knowing the constant presence of His divine friendship, God enables us to truly live out the social dimensions of loving our neighbor with a passionate outward love for others.

## Chapter 8

# Yahweh's Ten Loving Instructions

## Loving Your Neighbor–His Words Five to Ten

*While* the first four commandments establish the foundations for man's vertical relationship for loving God, the last six commandments establish the foundations for man's horizontal relationships with his fellow man. When the first four commands of loving instructions of God are observed, man himself is touched by and held in God's love. This, in turn, enables man's capacities for loving his neighbor.

Our culture is aching for this love. The secular world has virtually eliminated the vertical dimension of loving God. And much of the church world has altered the order by placing the love of neighbor ahead of love for God. With man as the center and measure of everything, there is no longer any anchor for an ethical or moral center.

Ethics are in continuous flux, ever-evolving into a more "relevant" system for the present. Truth, moral principles, right and wrong, and real goodness are held captive to whatever societal opinion currently holds them to be. Once love for God is eliminated, or demoted to second place, the dynamic to love others is removed.

John, one of the most intimate friends Jesus had in his earthly life, writes, "We love each other as a result of his loving us first."[104]

---

[104] I Jn 4:19. (NLT)

This is the reason why our present "modern" attempt at social ethics fails so miserably. There simply is no power to love in secular ethics. Nor is there any directional compass pointing to true moral north. Man who is separated from the love of God has neither the ability nor the moral direction required to love his neighbor in a meaningful way.

Thankfully, there is a divine logic embedded in the structure of the ten words of loving instructions that God graciously gave to His people. When the first things are assigned priority, second things naturally follow rather than being suppressed. Loving God with all of our hearts is the starting point for breaking the corruption of techno man's self-absorption and replacing it with a healing morality—including the love of our neighbor.

Obeying the first four commandments produces a deep love for God. And the development of our vertical love for God gives us the ability to express horizontal love to others. Thus, loving God is the gateway to loving others and the key to all proper ethics and conduct.

Commands five to ten become pertinent for every relationship man has with his neighbor, affecting every social institution and the structure of society itself. The relevance of these commands for addressing the endemic failures in the educational arena cannot be overstated. These foundations of human respect, dignity, and behavior—when taught by parents in their own homes—establish the moral principles that will maximize the potential for learning, achievement, and accomplishment in the lives of their children.

In the last six of God's loving instructions, He graciously gives us the moral direction we need for expressing a genuine love for others in all of our social relationships.

The first of these last six loving instructions focuses on how love is to be communicated to each other in family relationships, while the remaining five instructions chart a practical course for loving our neighbor.

### *FIVE*

The fifth loving instruction shifts from the vertical dimension of loving God to the horizontal sphere of loving others.

"***You***...honor your father and mother. Then you will live a long, full life in the land the LORD your God will give you."[105]

The philosophies of relativism and materialism in the late '60s aimed to destroy the existence of God, thereby destroying the vertical dimension of love for God for many in 21st century America. In this new millennium, the nuclear family, which is the basic social unit of all society and culture, has become the target for total annihilation. The traditional, nuclear family has taken direct hits from academia, politics, pop culture, and especially the media. Television sitcoms portray parents as dull-witted and incompetent. Their "brilliant" but irreverent children are, of course, the vehicles of logic and good sense.

The fruit of this subversion of authority has ripened and now is being practiced in the classroom. In some schools, teachers have found they simply cannot teach. Almost any classroom teacher in either public or private education, when asked what the most significant challenge to accomplishing their teaching goals are, will readily cite *discipline in the classroom*.

But as stated previously, discipline is a character, not an academic, issue. How can any qualified teacher accomplish his educational objectives with his students when his energy and time must be spent struggling to create a disciplined environment?

A few moments of reflection by any thoughtful person should sensibly lead to the recognition that it is the breakdown in

[105] Exod. 20:12. (NLT)

character and morality that has produced most of the issues of today. Will additional officers on the streets resolve the issue of street crime by deterring the violence of abandoned youth? Is this the solution for those who have been nurtured on a steady diet of killer heroes as role models via video and cinema in the absence of caring and loving parents who could have taught them the dignity of human life, particularly the value of their own lives? Why do an absent father and unfaithful husband much more likely subject their wives and children to poverty and possible delinquent behavior than one who stays at home caring for his family? Such a moral breakdown at home results in social issues that must be faced by the broader community.

The fifth loving instruction of honoring your father and mother provides the bridge to begin to resolve this dilemma. It is a commandment that first establishes the foundation for the right kind of-relationships and discipline in the home. Once established in the home environment, these proper relationships will be transferred and applied to the expanded fabric of social relations and governmental structures throughout society. Nowhere can be found a more relevant word from God, which, if applied, offers a cure for the moral malaise of our culture. This promise also provides the means to reverse the tragic loss of academic achievement taking place in the educational system today. Obedient children are a blessing to parents *and* a national treasure.

The fifth commandment is the first of God's loving instructions that comes with a built-in promise. "Honor your father and mother. If you honor your father and mother, *you will live a long life, full of blessing.*"[106] The promise for obeying this instruction is long life and emotional well-being.

What does it mean to honor one's parents? The root of the Hebrew word "honor" means heavy or weighty. Thus, to honor

---

[106] Eph. 6:3. (NLT)

one's parents is to give weight to them or esteem and respect them. Honor, during the early childhood years, is manifested primarily through obedience—or more accurately, submission—and service to parents. In Ephesians 6:1, Paul writes, "Children, obey your parents because you belong to the Lord, for this is the right thing to do." This is expanded in Colossians 3:20, "You children must always obey your parents, for this is what pleases the Lord."

Today such obedience is not in fashion. To even mention such a concept is exceptionally countercultural. Every effort is being made to lower the age of autonomy so that even preschoolers can pursue unbridled freedom. Our popular culture views any restraint as an assault on individual freedom, and obedience is considered mindless conformity.

But there is nothing senseless in the New Testament command to obey. To obey means to "listen under," that is, conscious listening. This is precisely the same wholehearted commitment to biblical hearing to which parents are first called, as described in Chapter 4. The central idea is to listen with the intent to understand and to obey. The rules are precisely the same for parents as they are for their children. The starting point of biblical obedience begins with parents in their relationship with God. Obeying God, first in their own lives, brings them into the love of God, which puts them into the proper position to exercise loving authority to instruct and discipline their children.

I have observed that many parents are unable to establish obedience in the lives of their children because they are actively resisting the authority of God and His rule in their own lives. Such parents often fail to understand why their children do not respect them and submit to their authority. It is because, as God's children, parents and their children are called to submit to the same rules of His loving authority. Parents cannot live unrighteous lives, rebel against God's authority in their own lives, and then expect their children to respect and obey them. Children quickly recognize such a hypocritical lifestyle and simply feed off the hidden rebellion in the lives of their parents, despite parents' efforts to cultivate obedience in their children.

Ephesians 6:1 states that children are to obey their parents "in the Lord," in other words, in those things that are consistent with His word. This does not mean that children are to obey their parents if they are directed to do something that is morally wrong or is contrary to Scripture or conscience. Wholehearted obedience is not mindless obedience. It is an exercise of freedom to choose and then do the right thing.

A disobedient spirit is intrinsically enslaving. The purpose of the redemptive coming of Jesus was to set men free from corrupting enslavements. Thus, in the early years, parents, in a sense, stand in place of God to their children. Under God's rule in their own lives, parents will generally have their children's best interest at heart as they establish boundaries for loving and living together as a family.

There is also a warning to fathers to carefully apply discipline to their children within a genuine framework of relational love for their children. Arbitrary authority can be hurtful, as described in Ephesians 6:4. "And now a word to you fathers. Do not make your children angry by the way you treat them. Rather, bring them up with the discipline and instruction approved by the Lord."

Dave Simmons, in his book, *Dad the Family Mentor,* paraphrases this same verse by saying, "Fathers, don't use a command style that frustrates your children and incites them to rebel against you and your value system automatically and spin out of control. Instead, use God's wisdom, be personally involved, and use proper command style to nourish them up with biblical principles of discipline and motivation."[107] Healthy submission and loving rela-

---

[107] Simmons, *Dad the Family Mentor*, 188.

tionships established in the home become foundations that will be carried into the broader context of loving one's neighbor outside the home for the rest of children's lives.

As childhood gives way to adulthood, the demonstration of honor changes in emphasis from *obedience* to *respect*. Such high regard for one's parents is even linked with the Sabbath and therefore seen as essential for living. "Each of you must show respect for your mother and father, and you must always observe my Sabbath days of rest, for I, the LORD, am your God."[108] This respect will be conveyed practically in affectionate verbal communication *to* and *about* one's parents. Concern (and involvement when necessary) for the material provisions for one's parents also express a genuine respect for them. Taking time to include parents in plans and spending time with them are acts of kindness that show respect. These actions also return the blessing for so many sacrificial acts made by loving parents for their children during the childhood years.

Perhaps the greatest return of honor and respect to parents a son or daughter can provide for their parents after leaving home are by the grown child's character and reputation. Proverbs 23:24-25 states, "The father of godly children has cause for joy. What a pleasure it is to have wise children. So, give your parents joy! May she who gave you birth be happy."

Joy, pleasure, and happiness! What more fabulous gifts of reverence and respect could be given than these to parents in their later years by the manner of life and character displayed in their children as they grow and mature? The giving of honor to parents by their children from early childhood into adulthood assures longevity and wellness throughout all of life for children while bringing joy and happiness to parents.

---

[108] Lev 19:3. (NLT)

Honor and respect for one's parents establish the foundation for honor and respect in all relationships in the whole social structure beyond the home as well. What incredible rewards await those who follow the fifth loving instruction given to us by God.

## *SIX*

The sixth loving instruction establishes the immense value of human life.

"***You***...shall not murder."[109]

Human life is precious, the value of life incalculable.

No previous age comes close to ours in the horror of killing. Homicide, suicide, murder, children dying at the hands of abusive parents, and feticide have led to the death of a multitude of lives. As of January 2020, National Right to Life estimates that 61,628,584 babies' lives have ended through legal abortion in the 47 years since the Supreme court ruling of Roe vs. Wade on January 22, 1973.[110] Terrorism promotes death throughout the earth. Our senses have been dulled and our minds seared to the tragedy of the loss of life around us. There is a murderous spirit on a rampage, making this the century of death.

The sixth commandment, if understood in its Scriptural depth and applied, will bring healing to the world around us. It consists of only two words giving a blunt imperative: "no murder!" Every life is of inestimable worth because man is created in God's image. Because man has rejected God he has unwittingly undermined his own value as well.

---

109 Exod. 20:13.

110 "State of Abortion in the United States." (January 22, 2020). National Right to Life Releases 7th Annual Report on NRLC. https://www.nrlc.org/communications/releases/2020/0122saus

Though we all continue to be astounded by the explosion of knowledge about our universe and observe the unveiling of God's handiwork, there remains the wonder of His chief work: the creation of man. "So God created people in His own image; God patterned them after himself; male and female he created them."[111] All men are created in the image of God.

Genesis 9:6 states, "Yes, you must execute anyone who murders another person, for to kill a person is to kill a living being made in God's image." A newborn child is an absolute wonder, born with a delicate moral sensibility and incomprehensible possibilities for achievement. And he or she is not only a human body but an eternal soul. Man is the apex of God's creation. Murder is not only a crime against mankind, it is a crime against God Himself in whose image we have been created.

Jesus said in Matthew 22:39 to "Love your neighbor as yourself." We are under divine obligation to cherish our neighbor's life as much as we admire our own. Because we have come to cherish God little, who has made us like Himself, we have ceased to cherish human life itself.

God has invested priceless worth in those He has formed and brought to life by the breath of His Spirit. This was twice demonstrated. First at creation, and then at our redemption when He gave up His own life at His cruel and unjust crucifixion to reclaim us for Himself. How valuable we are to Him! As a genuine love for God is formed within our hearts, love for ourselves, our neighbor, and the invaluable worth of human life become the heart of our whole moral ethic and lifestyle. When we once again catch a real glimpse of the value of human life from God's perspective, all of life, from conception to the grave, will be regarded with love and affection rather than targeted for murder.

---

111 Gen 1:27. (NLT)

Jesus plumbed the depth of this commandment by saying, "You have heard that the law of Moses says, 'Do not murder. If you commit murder, you are subject to judgment.' But I say, if you are angry with someone, you are subject to judgment! If you call someone an idiot, you are in danger of being brought before the high council. And if you curse someone, you are in danger of the fires of hell."[112] It is so easy to be a secret murderer in our minds and hearts. Treasured thoughts of anger and revenge toward others are as foul as murder.

The indwelling power of the Holy Spirit opens the channels for forgiveness and releases the ability to experience the total fulfillment of this healing commandment within us. What a winsome fruit this can become in our lives for those around us. The attitudes of our hearts that are expressed by our words and actions will inevitably form our children's view of worth for themselves and their neighbors. Will they have been touched through our communication and actions toward them in such a manner that they will have learned from us how valuable their life is, as someone who has been created in God's image? Will they witness our road rage when someone cuts us off in traffic as we drive them to school, or will they recognize that we view our neighbor as an individual created in God's image, though perhaps momentarily flawed?

The sixth instruction of Yahweh, which states, "do not murder," really teaches us about the value of life. Like all of God's commandments, this one will be a fountain of life to our neighbor when it is understood and lived out in our own life. Following this commandment of valuing life becomes part of the legacy of our hearts, which we will impart by God's grace to our children.

---

112 Matt 5:21-22. (NLT)

## *SEVEN*

To guard His precious gift of intimate companionship and joyous fulfillment of a physical, sexual relationship between male and female, God gave the seventh commandment,

"***You***...do not commit adultery."[113]

Muddled morality has produced complete confusion, broken lives, and is bringing physical death to vast numbers of people. God's will for man has always been to provide him with clarity for living to achieve maximum enjoyment, satisfaction, and well-being in all of life and relationships. Since God created male and female, His intention from the beginning for them has included the wondrous joys and pleasures which He designed and intended in human sexuality.

The joys of sex reach their zenith only as they are enfolded in the trusting relationship between a man and woman in the fidelity of married love. At creation, God created marriage, affirming the dignity and purity of this relationship. The fall did not create passion. It only perverted it.

Genesis 2:18 states, "It is not good for man to be alone." God created man and woman as social beings. Adam and Eve were partners for life. They were to be companions living with the richness of all of life shared as one. Underlying this relationship was a *covenant bond.* Unlike the temporary and shallow feeling-based relationships of our culture, real marriage and love are based on a commitment rather than on a fleeting passion. The marriage union was founded on a pledge of fidelity. In this marriage bond, children are a fruit of that relationship and a gift from God.[114] The very first of the 613 commandments found in

[113] Exod. 20:14. (NLT)

[114] Ps. 127:3-5 states, "Children are a gift from the LORD; they are a reward from him. Children born to a young man are like sharp arrows in a warrior's

the Old Testament was God's commandment for Adam and Eve to be fruitful and multiply.[115]

Proverbs 18:22 says, "The man who finds a wife finds a treasure and receives favor from the LORD." In the first part of the marriage ceremony in early rabbinic literature, the act of setting a couple aside in betrothal is known as *kiddushin* or *qiddushin*, an act of sanctification or consecration. The underlying meaning of the term *kiddushin* is to "be set apart," "to be holy." Thus, from the Hebrew perspective, marriage is a "sacred bond," "a holy relationship," "an act of being set apart unto God and each other."

This holy union carries the same calling which Israel received at Mt. Sinai to be a "holy nation."[116] Marriage is to be a visual replica of God's eternal covenant relation to His chosen bride (His holy people). This permanent betrothal love bond consummates in the marriage of Messiah with His bride, which will last forever! Marriage is a lifelong covenant, an exclusive commitment, and a word of promise that is kept.[117]

Children drink deeply as well from the companionship and permanent love bond that is shared between their parents as a committed husband and wife. Adultery violates this holy relationship and shatters the trust that establishes, nurtures, and sustains deep emotional and sexual intimacy for the parents. Broken

---

hands. How happy is the man whose quiver is full of them! He will not be put to shame when he confronts his accusers at the city gates."

[115] Gen. 1:28.

[116] Exod. 19:6.

[117] There is no special term in Biblical Hebrew for the term promise. The word *dabar* which means "word," "speech," or "commandment" is also the word used for promise. When *dabar* is rendered "promise" it implies something of substance—it was a pledge of one's good faith or promise to keep that word by pragmatic action. Simply stated, a promise in Biblical Hebrew was another way of saying that one was as good as one's word. Joshua 21:45 illustrates the use of "word" as "promise." "Not one of the good promises which the LORD had made to the house of Israel failed; all came to pass." (NAS)

marriages wound children as profoundly as they do husbands and wives.[118]

God deeply cherishes His creation and the holy relationship which He intended for man and woman to enjoy with each other. This loving commandment preserves this sacred union and conveys profound lessons into the hearts of observant children regarding the *nature of love* (a permanent bond), *commitment* (working together through all of life's pressures), and *keeping a promise* (the value of keeping one's word). This commandment was given by God to protect and preserve the wholeness and well-being of the sacred and lasting union between husband and wife.

## *EIGHT*

God's eighth commandment simply is,

"***You***...don't steal."[119]

Stealing is the natural human condition and presently rages in our culture. We all manage to find justification for our subtle acts of thievery. Taking something from others subtly and overtly is endemic. Workers rob employers of time and materials, while employers rob workers of adequate wages and safe working environments. When I was working at a hardware store during high school, I stole a knife that I desperately wanted from my employer. (Later in college, God helped me restore this wrong.)

We camouflage our breaking this commandment by replacing the word steal with "borrowed." Another popular word that has robbed our vocabulary of the clear moral meaning of steal, is "ripped off." We all miss the mark.

---

[118] Matthew Kalman writes about the depression that children of divorce experience in his editorial in *USA Today*. Feb. 17, 1999.

[119] Exod. 20:15.

Because the intrinsic value of human life has tragically been removed from our culture, one's "worth" is presently perceived to consist of the labels of one's clothes and the material possessions one has. A few years ago, in Norfolk, just north of where we lived, a high schooler was murdered by a fellow student because the student wanted his classmate's jacket! The lie perpetuated in cinema, television, and online is that life's primary goal is to get.

The unfortunate outcome of all theft is the undermining of respect for all personal property, without which society as we have known it will collapse. The ultimate welfare of society is at stake in the keeping or failure in the keeping of this loving instruction given by God for every man's good. Theft leads to compromise, which quickly becomes a habit. Like cancer, even a small theft can grow into total malignancy of character.

The anecdote for this natural character flaw within us all is complete regeneration by the redemptive work of God's spirit in our hearts. As God's children, we receive a transformed nature that is characterized by *giving* rather than taking. John 3:16 reveals the essential nature of God, "For God so loved the world that he *gave* his one and only Son, that whoever believes in him shall not perish but have eternal life." (NIV)[emphasis added]

God so loved the world that He *gave*!

With God's nature implanted in our hearts, we too will be givers. In giving, we will be spared from the inevitable corruption that results from stealing. Our children need to learn the nature of God's love in us by observing our lifestyle, which gives, rather than takes from others.

## *NINE*

"***You***...shall not give false testimony against your neighbor."[120]

Truth! What heartache our nation could have been spared over these last few years if this commandment would have been followed in private conduct and public office.

Initially focused against perjuring oneself in a judicial trial, lying in any form is addressed in Leviticus 19:11, which states, "... Do not lie. Do not deceive one another." (NIV) We have become a culture of liars. Politics, propaganda, and image are everything. When I speak to others about any lawful standard, I often receive uncomprehending looks. Cultural relativism is the dominant philosophy of our day. To most, truth is relative. But it is not.

To lie as a witness against someone else reveals the sickness of humankind. False accusations that tarnish someone else's character to preserve our reputation shows our total self-centeredness as well as our complete bankruptcy of love for our neighbor.

The absence of honesty in relationships breeds deceit and the destruction of all social institutions, both private and public. Deceit removes our lives from reality. The deep rebellion toward God in men's hearts has motivated massive efforts to deny His existence and the authority of His word. With God and His word removed from any practical application to human life and behavior, humanity proceeds on the path of self-deception to its own hurt.

The truth is that "The LORD detests lying lips, but he delights in men who are truthful."[121] God hates all falsehood because He is the Father of truth and because He is against all the strategies of Satan, whose ultimate aim is to destroy man. It is because God profoundly cares for man's well-being and desires fellowship with

---

[120] Exod. 20:16. (NIV)

[121] Prov 12:22. (NIV)

man that He hates lies. Any falsehood will not allow a man to stand in God's presence.[122]

Biblical learning calls for loving and radical truthfulness. Why? Because integrity is the pathway to growth and wholeness. Paul writes about this process in Ephesians 4:15, "...we will hold to the truth in love, becoming more and more in every way like Christ, who is the head of his body, the church. Under his direction, the whole body is fitted together perfectly. As each part does its special work, it helps the other parts grow, so that the whole body is healthy and growing and full of love." (NLT)

The truth may hurt. But truth spoken in love ultimately brings healing and health. Biblical learning produces wholeness and purity of character. Emotional health is the result of inner cleansing. As Jesus neared the end of His earthly ministry, His prayer for us was, "Make them pure and holy by teaching them your words of truth."[123] He prayed this way for us because He genuinely loves us and cares for us.

As models for our children, our own lives need to exhibit honesty and truthfulness in our relationships with God, our spouses, our children, and our neighbors. Ponder for a moment what the outcome would be for our national health and well-being if this were the pathway followed by all. Truth in relationships will be

---

122 God is faithful and true. Jesus came to reveal the nature of the invisible God. In John 14:6, Jesus simply says, "I am the...truth" and of his Father's word Jesus says, "Your word is truth." (John 17:17) In regard to the nature of Satan, John 8:44 says, "He was a murderer from the beginning, not holding to the truth, for there is no truth in him. When he lies, he speaks his native language, for he is a liar and the father of lies. (NIV). Psalm 101:7 warns, "I will not allow deceivers to serve me, and liars will not be allowed to enter my presence." (NLT)

123 John 17:17. (NLT)

operative if we genuinely love our neighbor. Truth is the core of genuine biblical learning.

## *TEN*

The last loving instruction brings us full circle to address our interior lives, just as the first commandment did.

This loving word from God says,

"***You***...do not covet your neighbor's house. Do not covet your neighbor's wife, male or female servant, ox or donkey, or anything else your neighbor owns."[124]

The first commandment admonishes us to plumb the priority of love for God *in our hearts*. The last loving word given to us in the tenth commandment explores the depth of our love for our neighbor. It cuts to the core of the invisible domain in all our hearts by admonishing us to evaluate our hidden attitude toward our neighbors.

The Hebrew word *hamad* (covet) means "strong desire, specifically to an excessive, ungoverned, selfish desire." In a word, to covet is to have greed (lust) for what does not rightfully belong to us. One of the most gripping and all-encompassing powers that characterizes the culture of our time is greed. No one has enough of their own stuff. Lust is a disease that drives people to sacrifice everything, including marriage and family, in a perpetual race in a vain effort to obtain an elusive goal. People desire other's possessions, spouses, status, and lifestyles. Covetousness is an invisible cancer of attitude that assaults fellow humans. This lust is self-serving and self-loving.

Covetousness is the hidden power that leads to the breaking of the last six of God's commandments, all of which have to do with loving one's neighbor as oneself. In Proverbs 21:26, Solomon

---

[124] Exod. 20:17. (NLT)

draws the distinguishing difference in attitude between righteous and evil people, "They are always greedy for more, while the godly love to give!" (NLT) The pursuit of "stuff" robs men of some of the most meaningful, rewarding, and satisfying aspects of being created in God's image. Covetousness makes it impossible to love one's neighbor.

Jesus, in his love for a covetous young man in Luke 12:15, warned him from falling into the deceitful pathway of greed by saying, "Beware! Do not be greedy for what you don't have. Life is not measured by how much we own."[125] There are greater riches than that which can be seen in the visible world, like the priceless reformation of heart and character. First Timothy 6:6 states, "But godliness [actually] is a means of great gain when accompanied by contentment." (NAS) The *New Living Testament* translates the meaning of this same verse as follows, "Yet true religion with contentment is great wealth." Contentment is a gift that comes from God. Such contentment brings wholeness and liberation from greed's grasp on our inner being.

Covetousness is enslaving. One of the invaluable gifts God gives us as His children is that we are liberated from the unrest of ceaseless covetousness. Jesus said, "But seek first his kingdom and his righteousness, and all these things will be given to you as well." (NIV) As our interior life is filled with God, His love *for* us flows *from* us to loving our neighbors, and we are set free from being chronic takers into becoming generous givers.

Gratitude will become our inner wellspring as we perceive God's abundant provisions for all of life. As our children observe our acts of kindness and partake in our thankful spirits, they will

---

[125] (NLT). The New American Standard Bible translates the same verse, "Beware, and be on your guard against every form of greed; for not *{even}* when one has an abundance does his life consist of his possessions." See Luke 12:13-31 where Jesus addresses the whole issue of covetousness in a wonderful parable.

experience God's riches that come with generous, grateful attitudes of the heart. These are priceless gifts we can give our children from the legacy of our hearts in a world held captive by greed. God gives us this loving instruction to rescue us from the tyranny of a coveting heart.

Surprisingly, the primary focus up to this point for establishing a foundation for biblical learning for our children has been on us as parents rather than our children. The reason for this is simple yet profound. As parents, we are commanded to teach our children the truth about God. Our manner of life is intended by God to be the means to equip our children to know God and know how to make Him known. God has structured family relationships to facilitate this process of generational parenting, and graciously provided the guidelines for accomplishing this goal.

In Psalm 78:1-7, King David recognized and reiterated this generational imperative first given by God in Deuteronomy chapter 6. David writes, "Listen, O my people, to my instruction; incline your ears to the words of my mouth. I will open my mouth in a parable; I will utter dark sayings of old, which we have heard and known, and our fathers have told us. We will not conceal them from their children but tell the generation to come of the praises of the LORD, and His strength and the wondrous works that He has done. For He established a testimony in Jacob and appointed a law in Israel, which He *commanded* our fathers, that they should teach them to their children, that the generation to come might know, [even] the children [yet] to be born, [that] they may arise and tell [them] to their children, that they should put their confidence in God, and not forget the works of God, but keep His commandments." [emphasis added] The law that God appointed in Israel was that the primary responsibility for transferring biblical learning to children was delegated to parents and that it should be implemented so effectively that biblical learning and biblical lifestyles would be perpetuated *for four generations!* Parents are the foundation of God's plan for creating and sustaining a holy nation. His plan has not changed.

The heart of authentic biblical learning for our children is founded upon our own transformed hearts, character, and lifestyle as parents.[126] Our character and behavior provide living examples, which express the nature of God and the practical goodness of God's loving instructions as they have been written in our hearts and practiced in our day-to-day living, which is observed by our children.

Psalm 119 records a beautiful song that expresses King David's heart toward God and his attitude and respect for His loving instructions. I pray these words will help shape our love for God and affection for His word in our pursuit to become competent and skilled teachers of real biblical learning in the lives of our children.

## David's Song

"You have charged us to keep your commandments carefully. Oh, that my actions would consistently reflect your principles! Then I will not be disgraced when I compare my life with your commands. When I learn your righteous laws, I will thank you by living as I should! I will obey your principles. Please don't give up on me! ***How can a young person stay pure? By obeying your word and following its rules.*** I have tried my best to find you—don't let me wander from your commands. I have hidden your word in my

[126] The importance of this principle bears repeating. The essence of authentic biblical education *begins with parents*, *not* children. Children learn best by what they see demonstrated, *then* taught by their own parents. Notice this order in Deut 6:6-7, "And *you must commit yourselves wholeheartedly to these commands* I am giving you today. *(Then)* Repeat them again and again to your children. Talk about them when you are at home and when you are away on a journey, when you are lying down and when you are getting up again. (NLT)

heart, that I might not sin against you. Blessed are you, O LORD; teach me your principles. I have recited aloud all the laws you have given us. I have rejoiced in your decrees as much as in riches. I will study your commandments and reflect on your ways. I will delight in your principles and not forget your word. Be good to your servant, that I may live and obey your word. ***Open my eyes to see the wonderful truths in your law. I am but a foreigner here on earth; I need the guidance of your commands. Don't hide them from me!*** I am overwhelmed continually with a desire for your laws. You rebuke those cursed proud ones who wander from your commands. Don't let them scorn and insult me, for I have obeyed your decrees. Even princes sit and speak against me, but I will meditate on your principles. Your decrees please me; they give me wise advice. I lie in the dust, completely discouraged; revive me by your word. I told you my plans, and you answered. Now teach me your principles. ***Help me understand the meaning of your commandments, and I will meditate on your wonderful miracles.*** I weep with grief; encourage me by your word. ***Keep me from lying to myself; give me the privilege of knowing your law.*** I have chosen to be faithful; I have determined to live by your laws. I cling to your decrees. LORD, don't let me be put to shame! If you will help me, I will run to follow your commands. Teach me, O LORD, to follow every one of your principles. ***Give me understanding and I will obey your law; I will put it into practice with all my heart.*** Make me walk along the path of your commands, for that is where my happiness is found. ***Give me an eagerness for your decrees; do not inflict me with love for money! Turn my eyes from worthless things, and give me life through your word.*** Reassure me of your promise, which is for those who honor you. Help me abandon my shameful ways; your laws are all I want in life. I long to obey your commandments! ***Renew my life with your goodness.*** LORD, give to me your unfailing love, the salvation that you promised me. Then I will have an answer for those who taunt me, for I trust in your word. Do not snatch your word of truth from me, for my only hope is in your laws. I will keep on obeying your law forever and forever. ***I will walk in freedom, for I have devoted myself to your commandments.*** I will speak to kings about your decrees, and I will not be ashamed. ***How I delight in your commands! How I love them!*** (Ps. 119:4-47) [emphasis added]

The outcome of understanding and walking in God's commandments leads to an exceptional quality of life—for parents and their children!

**The outcome of understanding and walking in God's commandments is unsurpassed quality of life and freedom!**

Part 3

# Foundations Unlocked –at Home

CHAPTER 9

# At Home

## Putting It All Together

*As* the love of God flows in our hearts through our relationship with Him, our obedience to His loving instructions leads us into a quality of life and a holy lifestyle that is satisfying, real, and emotionally whole. We will be walking along the pathway that will place and keep us in the most advantageous place to train, instruct, and lead our children into authentic biblical learning.

**If you want to change the world, go home, and love your family.**
**- Mother Teresa**

We all have free will. We choose our values and priorities and ultimately do what we want to do. Excelling in parenting requires a decision. God gives us our children as His gifts. The priceless gift of time is also one of God's gifts. We have our children for a season. How we steward the moments we spend in raising them will affect their well-being, learning capacities, life contributions, and final spiritual destiny for eternity.

God's plan is for children to be nurtured, trained, and instructed in biblical truth while immersed in the relational love bond between their parents as husband and wife. As well, the relationship we as parents have established with God, including our reception of His loving instructions, is to be communicated and imparted to our children during their childhood years.

Abraham, who became the father of faith for all those who believe in God, was chosen because of his relationship to God. One reason God called Abraham His friend was because God knew Abraham would command (train) his children. "I have chosen him for a reason, namely that he will carefully instruct his children and his household to keep themselves strong in relationship to Me and to walk in My ways by doing what is good and right in the world and by showing mercy and justice to all others. I know he will uphold his end of the covenant so that he can ensure My promises to him will be fulfilled and upheld as well."[127] Not only did Abraham know God, but God knew him! God saw the integrity of Abraham's character.

How will biblical learning become the legacy of our children as well as our own? What are the primary psychological and emotional needs that our children have that must be met by us during this process that will fill them with peace[128] and become the foundation for their capacities for learning and living?

There are at least four essential elements that we must provide to meet these needs, which in turn help to establish all the biblical learning capacities we desire to be resident in our children.

---

[127] Gen. 18:19.

[128] Please see Chapter 2, footnote 28 for a complete description of peace (*shalom*).

These vital elements constitute the core and fabric of what I have chosen to call *relational learning*. Each is rooted in God and the government of God.

These relational building blocks in biblical learning have little to do with the commonly recognized aspects of formal education. Nevertheless, when the essential four relational learning elements are understood and consistently applied by parents, biblical learning will occur in the lives of our children, enhancing their capacities for learning in all realms to help them reach their fullest potential. I call these four building blocks *relational elements* of biblical learning because the substance of every one of these vital foundations has its origin and finds its fulfillment in a loving relationship with a person rather than in a book.

The foundations for biblical learning must begin from the inside (heart) and work their way out. All of life and learning starts deep in the heart, works its way through character and out to behavior. If a person's heart is right, his character will be sound. If a person's character is sound, acceptable behavior will follow, and the capacities for life and learning will reach maximum fulfillment.

BIOS is the term used to describe the internal operating system of a computer. More specifically, BIOS stands for Basic Input/Output System. It functions as the invisible but vital intermediary between a computer's hardware and software. If the BIOS is faulty, the finest computer (hardware) and programs (software) will be useless. A computer will not function correctly without a properly functioning BIOS.

A computer system can serve as a picture of learning. The hardware may be likened to all the physical abilities, intellectual, and genetic capacities that a person may possess. The software may be likened to the unlimited array of environmental factors, educational tools, and learning curriculums available to the learner. The BIOS can be likened to the heart[129] of the learner.

In the learning process, an individual's BIOS (heart) is continuously acting as the basic input/output system. The invisible but real internal operating system (the *inner self* that thinks, feels, and decides) serves as the constant intermediary between a learner's physical *abilities* (with all the learning materials) and a learner's *experiences*.

Because a learner's BIOS (heart) is little understood and overlooked by educators, many attempts to achieve satisfactory educational outcomes are deeply flawed. For example, very young children may be exposed to formal learning environments and material before their own BIOS has developed to the point of being able to properly process the requirements (emotional and intellectual content) of the particular learning situation. This would be like attempting to flip the switch of a Pentium computer on to run outstanding computer software without finishing the installation of the internal operating system (BIOS). The outcome would be muddled at best, or utterly disastrous at its worst. Without proper regard for the development of a preschoolers' BIOS (heart), many early learning approaches may be flawed at their inception.

In other learning situations, some gifted learners are offered the finest and most advanced curriculums with apparently dismal learning outcomes. Why? Even though these talented learners may exhibit high IQs, their BIOS (hearts) may be dysfunctional or crippled. In such situations, does changing the curriculum provide the solution to enhancing the learning outcome, or is restoring the correct functioning of a learner's BIOS (heart) the *real* solution to improving the learning outcome?

---

[129] Please see Chapter 1, footnote 7 for a discussion of all of the characteristics and nature of the heart.

Most educational approaches focus on either the hardware (the learner's abilities) or the software (teaching tools and curriculum) to produce desired learning outcomes. The learner's BIOS (heart) is omitted because of ignorance of its crucial role in learning. Man tests the mind or intellect. God tests our hearts.[130]

Therefore, in all authentic biblical learning, the BIOS (heart) of the learner is the first and continuing priority throughout the learning process. The inner being of the learner is the authentic biblical pathway to maximizing all the learning capacities of the student. The learner's inner being is also the doorway that allows the instructor to fulfill his/her educational goals for each learner. I have observed time and again that instructors are severely thwarted in their mission to deliver instruction in their area of expertise because of the faulty BIOS within the lives of many of the students. A poorly functioning BIOS (heart) disrupts and, in some instances, eliminates the possibility of instruction.

What are the primary ingredients that constitute relational learning? What must we provide that will meet the underlying psychological and emotional needs of our children and become the foundation for a sound heart (BIOS) in the lives of our children? What will produce the highest IQ (inner qualities) of the learner's BIOS?

There are volumes written about the following four essential elements that lead to wholeness of human personality, growth, maturity, and achievement. However, in our present culture, some

---

[130] Jer 11:20a states, "O LORD Almighty, you are just, and *you examine the deepest thoughts of hearts and minds.* (NLT) The Hebrew word *bachan* (try/examine) means to test, prove, try, or scrutinize and is used of gold, persons, and the heart. The Hebrew word *kilyah* (reins/deepest thoughts or feelings) is the same word used for our twin organs (kidneys) in the lower back which function to filter impurities from the blood. When used figuratively, this term (*kilyah*) refers to the innermost aspects of personality. In Psa. 26:2 David says, "Put me on trial, LORD, and cross-examine me. Test my motives and affections." (NLT). Also see Rev. 2:23.

of these relational building blocks have been lost and/or the meanings tragically altered. Each one of these primary building blocks is deserving of much more significant development and description. What follows is an initial effort to establish the biblical roots for these four basic building blocks for developing a healthy functioning BIOS for the learner.

The process for developing biblical learning in our children is based upon God's revelation of who we are as His unique creation. He has given us His instructions, as well, to help us fulfill this goal. Properly understood, these relational building blocks all contribute profound goodness for the learner. Applied and developed appropriately, these building blocks have an untold significance in contributing to what I call "preventative parenting." Most remedial educational efforts and social programs are designed to make up the difference for what learners need but failed to receive from their parents to help them develop a healthy functioning BIOS, especially in the early formative stages of childhood. Failures in the original process that God has provided result in crippling the hearts of learners (BIOS) and have forced the creation of a magnitude of costly financial, educational, and social programs in man's efforts to remediate this initial failure *at home*.

The four relational building blocks that we, as parents, must provide to help form and develop our children's hearts (BIOS) will be explored in Chapters 10 and 11. These building blocks provide the means for establishing strong close relationships, affection, and affirmation between parents and their children, leading to quality of life and wholehearted learning.

Chapter 10

# Love and Bonding

## Relational Foundations

*The* greatest need of the human heart is life (relationship), not knowledge. The four relational building blocks that we as parents must provide to help form and develop our children's hearts (BIOS) are *love, bonding, discipline,* and *mentoring*. God is creative. How we learn to apply these four foundational building blocks for the development of our children's BIOS will be creative as well.

Each building block is presented as a beginning threshold for exploration in the multidimensional journey that we experience with our children, *especially* when God is present. God has designed these vital relational building blocks to operate in the relationships we have with our children. He has taken great care to give us His instructions for establishing these foundations for authentic biblical learning in our children. Our understanding and timely application of these four relational building blocks with our children will form, develop, and help bring our children's hearts (BIOS) to maturity and become the foundations for wholehearted learning.

We do not need to be perfect in providing these foundations. We just need to be willing and consistent. As God's children, we are in a growth process with our heavenly Father who genuinely loves us. He is our source and guides in this adventure with our children as we grow in our relationship with Him together with our children.

Remember, in all authentic biblical learning, the development of the BIOS (heart) of the learner is the first and continuing priority throughout the learning process. God has designed this system to enable us as parents to pass who we are on to our children.

It is not an accident that family forces work as they do. Dysfunctional parents produce troubled children who grow up and start dysfunctional families. God's whole redemptive plan for man and families is to deposit His wholeness into human lives to bring maximum fulfillment in living and learning—God-honoring parents produce God-honoring children who grow up and nurture God-honoring families. God has given us, as parents, the privilege and responsibility of imparting a healthy heart to our children at home. God's design is for our children to receive the legacy of our hearts, which will become their operational BIOS for life, and the inheritance of their children's children as well.

## *LOVE*

In anticipation of His sacrificial death as the Lamb of God, Jesus made this statement to His closest friends, "Greater love has no one than this, that he lay down his life for his friends."[131] God's love for man resided in the heart of His only son, expressing itself in selfless action that benefited us profoundly and cost Him immensely. He exchanged his wholeness and holiness for our brokenness and corruption so that we could be forgiven and become like Him. Our significance and personal value have forever been established by the free offering of the Messiah's lifeblood for us. His example and our own experience of knowing His sacrificial love for us summons us into giving the same kind of love to our

---

[131] John 15:13.

children. Love is an action that will find its expression in very practical ways.

This kind of love is costly to our naturally self-centered lives. One of the most precious commodities that we have as parents is our time. We demonstrate our love for our children by giving both *quantities of* and *quality* time to them. Children think, "If Dad and Mom love me, they will spend time with me." How we allocate the spending of our discretionary time sends a clear signal to our children of their value and priority to us. Why do small children repeatedly ask the same questions and ask us to read the same stories to them over and over? It is not because they don't remember the answers or recall the storylines, but because these are their techniques to be with us. It is their invitation for us to satisfy their deep need for us to step into their lives and be a part of them. Quality time generally is not something that can simply be scheduled. Quality time usually is the result of those unexpected special moments of heart-to-heart intimacy we experience with our children amid the countless quantities of time we spend with them just hanging out. Quality time becomes those unplanned events in which our children open their hearts to drink deeply of our love for them and find answers to their searching questions.

The importance of how we spend our time inside our homes is often subverted and replaced by a false perception of our "worth" in our occupations outside our homes. God's design is that our careers help us serve our children rather than ourselves. Prominent corporations can dismiss top-level executives with little advance notice. In an instant, the total investment of one's life work ceases, and the "importance" of one's sacrificial efforts disappears, and sadly often not even missed. Not so in the home! Parents are irreplaceable in the lives of their children. Our priorities are demonstrated by the *choices* we make every day. By spending time with our children, the integrity of our words, "I love you" is established and verified. Giving up our time for the benefit of our children is costly. It is unselfish love in action.

God's love is also *unconditional*.[132] He demonstrates this practically by the way He nourishes, cherishes, and provides daily for all humanity and particularly for us as His children.[133] As a husband and father, I am to love my spouse and children with the same kind of love with which Jesus loves His children. Such profound love is unique and impossible for us to give as mere humans. We acquire this love out of the relationship God provides us with Himself, empowering us to begin to express God's love through

---

[132] Paul writes about this deep unconditional love in Rom 5:5-11. "And this expectation will not disappoint us. For we know how dearly God loves us, because he has given us the Holy Spirit to fill our hearts with his love. When we were utterly helpless, Christ came at just the right time and died for us sinners. Now, no one is likely to die for a good person, though someone might be willing to die for a person who is especially good. But God showed his great love for us by sending Christ to die for us while we were still sinners. And since we have been made right in God's sight by the blood of Christ, he will certainly save us from God's judgment. For since we were restored to friendship with God by the death of His Son while we were still his enemies, we will certainly be delivered from eternal punishment by His life. So now we can rejoice in our wonderful new relationship with God—all because of what our Lord Jesus Christ has done for us in making us friends of God." (NLT)

[133] As a wonderful creator God has taken full responsibility for His creation and cares for His creatures by providing all that man needs. God has made provision for man's physical needs with all that He created within the entire physical universe. (see Genesis 1:28-29) Since man has deep spiritual needs as well as physical needs (see Matthew 4:4) God has made every provision to meet these needs by giving us His word, by revealing Himself in Jesus Christ so that we might know Him, and by giving us the gift of His Holy Spirit so that we might become like Him from the inside out! In 2 Peter 1:2-3 Peter writes, "Grace and peace be yours in abundance through the knowledge of God and of Jesus our Lord. His divine power has given us everything we need for life and godliness through our knowledge of him who called us by his own glory and goodness."(NIV) God's love *in us* will motivate and enable us to *unconditionally* care for our children's physical and spiritual needs as well.

our lives. The Holy Spirit pours out this quality and kind of love in our hearts[134] and we can use it with our families.

Our children thirst for unconditional love from us. Recently a coworker of mine overheard the request of a neglected young child to a neighbor who often walked his dog, "Can I be your dog?" This young child had perceived that he would receive more love and affection from his neighbor as his dog than from his own family at home. The absence of this love in infancy and early childhood infects a child's BIOS with meaninglessness and worthlessness. A neglected child will think, "I am unworthy and lack value. If I were significant, I would have my parents' attention. There must be something wrong with me." The absence of unconditional love scars a child's sense of well-being and damages trust in relationships, trust that is paramount to all subsequent learning experiences.

One of the primary ways we demonstrate our unconditional love for our children is by giving them our affection. We can fill and keep our children's emotional tanks filled by giving them our affection, or we can withhold it and force our children into a chronic search for affection, which may lead them to partake in relationships and/or substances that will fill them with poison.

Paul's words are instructive to us about two ways to show affection. Paul writes, "Having thus a fond affection for you, we were well-pleased to impart to you not only the gospel of God but also our own lives because you had become very dear to us."[135] We

---

[134] In Romans 5:5, Paul writes, "For we know how dearly God loves us, because he has given us the Holy Spirit *to fill* our hearts with his love." In Greek the word to fill (*ekcheo*) means to pour forth or bestow, more precisely to gush out, run greedily out, shed, or spill. Thus we could say that the Holy Spirit becomes the constant source of supply in our hearts in order to enable us to *express* God's love to our children. What an outstanding provision God has given to us for this undertaking! He gives us *Himself*!

[135] I Thessalonians 2:8. (NAS)

demonstrate our genuine affection for our children by giving them 1) biblical truth, and 2) ourselves.

The impartation of biblical truth has already been extensively covered in previous chapters. Our obedience to God's word and all His loving instructions become the wellspring of life from which our children deeply drink as they observe our example confirming the integrity of God's word. Genuine affection, therefore, will include our concern for our children's spiritual well-being, resulting in the generous sharing of God's word (imparting biblical truth) with them through our words and actions.

We give ourselves away in affectionate love in the way we give *attention* to our children, how we *listen*, *communicate*, and *discipline.*[136]

For children, attention is an unusual commodity. The more that is given, the less they will need. The less that is shown, the more it will be demanded. Children will stop at nothing to have their legitimate need for attention filled. In the early years, generous amounts of attention do not spoil children but instead supply a genuine need. When this basic need has been fulfilled, children quickly occupy themselves with other expanding interests.

During the preschool ages with our children, Gretchen and I would sometimes encounter a few puzzling and unexpected discipline problems. As I reflected on some of these circumstances, I realized that some of the regular allotments of time with our children had been displaced with other activities that precipitated perceived "misbehavior." Once the usual need for attention was again supplied, the discipline problem was usually dissolved. Our children simply needed a little more of our time rather than correction.

How we listen to our children is another way we give our children attention and show our affection for them. Children are

---

[136] Discipline as one expression of our love is developed more fully in Chapter 11.

incredibly perceptive of how fully we are tuned in to their conversations with us. Have you ever been distracted and thinking about other matters while engaged in a conversation with a child? Children quickly notice and will grab hold of your head and turn it toward them for you to zero in on their conversation. It is so easy for us as parents to think that the internal affairs and all the "important" matters going on in our thoughts are of more value than the little person engaged in conversation with us. Our children often must help us refocus our attention on the importance of the matter at hand—them!

Listening is one form of love in action that builds their sense of significance. Giving material gifts is not a substitute. Children, without listening parents, experience the pain of rejection and feel like nonpersons. Children have a natural thirst for a relationship with us that can be filled by no other person or material possession. Genuine listening is one way we give ourselves to our children and satisfy this thirst.

How would any of us ever know, experience, or comprehend the love God has for us had He not communicated with us? The record of the remarkable life of Jesus in the New Testament gives us graphic word pictures of God's loving involvement with man through His only son. With His hands, Jesus touched lepers to make them whole. With His voice, He comforted His followers and commanded storms that threatened their lives to cease. Out of His resources, Jesus fed a multitude of hungry people. And from His heart, Jesus walked a pathway that led to His death for us. His whole life was a spectrum of His love visibly communicated to us.

Our children thrive on our verbal and nonverbal love communicated to them. They need to hear "I love you" and "I appreciate you" frequently. Compliment their mental, emotional, and spiritual traits that emphasize the inner person rather than external looks and beauty. Recognize and commend them for achievements while being careful not to convey that your love has been earned by their performance. Children need to be loved just as fully in their failures as in their successes.

Nonverbal love is demonstrated by how we affectionately touch and hug our children from infancy to maturity. Physically loving and devoted fathers produce chaste daughters and manly sons. Healthy physical attitudes are the result of generous doses of physical and nonverbal affection for our children.

One of the best things mothers and fathers can do for their children is to love each other visibly. Our children feel loved and secure when they see us demonstrate our affection and actively show our love to our spouses. In his early years, when our son Jonathan would see me hugging Gretchen at home, he would come over and try to wiggle right in between us. Sometimes we have a family hug where we all gather in a huddle, put our arms around each other, and then hug each other as tightly as we could. Being a bit shorter (which is no longer the case) than the rest of us, Jonathan squirmed and pushed his way in between us all until he could be in the very center of our love huddle.

(Note to dads: From the example of Christ's priesthood, fathers must learn to also actively love each member of the family as an intercessor on their behalf. Spiritual traffic must pass through Dad. As our high priest, Jesus not only offered Himself sacrificially for us in His death but now He continues in that capacity to pray for our benefit and safety.[137] What *we* dads do in this arena determines the destiny of our families! God's love for us was validated when He gave Himself up for us. Taking the time to watch, pray, and

---

[137] "But Jesus remains a priest forever; his priesthood will never end. Therefore he is able, once and forever, to save everyone who comes to God through him. He lives forever to plead with God on their behalf. He is the kind of high priest we need because he is holy and blameless, unstained by sin. He has now been set apart from sinners, and he has been given the highest place of honor in heaven." Heb 7:24-26 (NLT)

remain alert to the spiritual well-being of each family member is one of the ways we express our sacrificial love for them. We are God's representative for our household,[138] and our vigilance protects and guards the well-being of every family member.)

As our children grow, our involvement with them in their expanding array of interests, functions, and projects becomes one of the most practical expressions of our continuing love for them. How much difference is there in the performance of our daughter at her ballet recital or our son's basketball game when we are present to watch and to cheer for them? It is our presence that makes the difference, and that difference cannot be measured.

Love is also an attitude that colors our whole approach to raising our children. Philippians 2:5-8 describes this attitude, "Your attitude should be the same that Christ Jesus had. Though he was God, he did not demand and cling to his rights as God. He made himself nothing; he took the humble position of a slave

[138] Exodus 12 records the instructions which Yahweh gave Moses for the first Passover. Verses 3 and 23 say, "Tell the whole community of Israel that on the tenth day of this month each man is to take a lamb for his family, one for each household. . .When the LORD goes through the land to strike down the Egyptians, he will see the blood on the top and sides of the doorframe and will pass over that doorway, and he will not permit the destroyer to enter *your houses* and strike you down." (NIV) The principle revealed in this setting is that man has a unique role as head and covering over his entire household. The obedience of the head of each family during the Passover either assured the well-being of each family member or permitted destruction to enter. In the case of the Passover, failure to function in this priestly role resulted in the physical death of their first born child. God is a God of families. That is why family structure and government is so important for every family member to honor and understand. One other Scripture which illustrates this principle in the New Testament was the experience that Paul's jailer had that resulted in his entire *household* gaining entrance into God's kingdom. (see Acts 16:30-34) In God's kingdom we are all called to function as priests, but in the family, the father is given a unique role to be sentry and guard keeper of the entire household.

and appeared in human form. And in human form, he obediently humbled himself even further by dying a criminal's death on a cross."

God's sacrificial love—planted and experienced in our hearts as parents and then practically sewn into the hearts and lives of our children—becomes the *relational foundation* for our children's BIOS (heart) and learning. This love is multidimensional, practical, and real. Biblical love is an attitude of mind and heart that deliberately chooses to give the gift of self for the well-being of our children at a cost to ourselves regardless of the performance of our children. As God's love for us is translated into a love for our children, we will demonstrate to them a sacrificial, active, and unconditional love. God, Himself is our source and foundation for giving this kind of love[139] to our children.

**Biblical love is an attitude of mind and heart that deliberately chooses to give the gift of self for the benefit and well-being of our children at a cost to ourselves regardless of the performance of our children.**

[139] This kind of love is described in 1 Corinthians, 13:4-8, "Love is patient and kind. Love is not jealous or boastful or proud or rude. Love does not demand its own way. Love is not irritable, and it keeps no record of when it has been wronged. It is never glad about injustice but rejoices whenever the truth wins out. Love never gives up, never loses faith, is always hopeful, and endures through every circumstance. Love will last forever. . ." (NLT). This is the kind of love that is given to us through our *relationship* with Him.

From conception to maturity, the expression of this kind of love nurtures a deep sense of value in our children. As we humble ourselves and love our children, we assign significance to them. When we concentrate on our children rather than ourselves, we make *them* feel special. Unconditional love establishes the importance and worth of each family member. Love and acceptance remove the fear of rejection and creates a home environment that allows each of our children to develop positive self-esteem, build self-confidence, and blossom into full potential. During the early years, children understand more than they can express. They are like sponges soaking up our words, actions, and the atmosphere that we create out of our love for them.

Such love meets the deepest longing and need of all of humanity—the need to be genuinely loved and cared for. Psychological health and well-being are the rewards of our giving this kind of love to our children through each developmental stage of their lives.[140] Knowing and experiencing this kind of love becomes the bedrock of our children's BIOS (heart). The power and influence of these IQs (inner qualities) cannot be underestimated in building the best heart BIOS (basic input/output system) for all subsequent learning experiences.

## *BOND/ATTACHMENT*

In the magnificence and goodness of God's entire creation, God recognized one deficiency.

[140] There are extensive materials available that provide practical help for knowing and understanding what we need to do as parents during each particular developmental stage that our children will pass through on their journey to maturity. Being prepared to provide what is needed that is *age specific* during these growth phases becomes our translation of God's love to them which is communicated and expressed in a manner that our children understand. See the bibliography and further reading for many useful resources.

Adam was alone.

Even though no human failure or sin was marring the Edenic landscape at creation's beginning *and* even though God Himself had a relationship with Adam, God's assessment of the situation for Adam in Genesis 2:18 was, "It is not good that man should be alone; I will make him a help meet for him."(KJV)

Adam needed to belong to someone like himself. The Hebrew word *neged* in most translations is translated with the nebulous "I will make him a help *meet* for him." Strongs Concordance translates *neged* as a counterpart (exact resemblance) placed in Adam's presence.[141] In today's language, God was saying to Adam, "I will place one suitable and comparable to you in your face!" You might say it was instantaneous bonding at first sight.

Taking one of Adam's ribs (his essential nature), God formed Eve and then joined them together. Adam exclaimed, "At last! She is part of my flesh and bone! She will be called 'woman' because she was taken out of a man." This explains why a man leaves his father and mother and is joined to his wife, and the two are united into one.[142]

Adam did not just notice Eve. Adam encountered Eve! And her presence brought deep satisfaction to Adam. She met his yearning to love and be loved, to exchange knowledge and affection with one of his kind. This first marriage in human history was kindled with an indissoluble bond that was not ever to be severed. In this marriage bond, Adam and Eve shared an attachment of the purest and most perfect kind between equals of the same class. Together, they experienced profound closeness and intimacy. They belonged to each other. They were delighted with each other.

Solomon amplified the assessment of Adam's deep need for companionship and attachment as he applied it to all men, "Two

---

[141] James Strong. #5048. The Exhaustive Concordance of the Bible.

[142] Gen 2:23-24. (NLT)

people can accomplish more than twice as much as one; they get a better return for their labor. If one person falls, the other can reach out and help. But people who are alone when they fall are in real trouble. And on a cold night, two under the same blanket can gain warmth from each other. But how can one be warm alone? A person standing alone can be attacked and defeated, but two can stand back-to-back and conquer. Three are even better, for a triple-braided cord is not easily broken."[143]

Fulfilling the core human need for bonding and attachment (to feel a part of someone else) is essential for the development of the psychological and emotional well-being of a child. Early bonding is vital to the whole internal learning process (BIOS) from infancy to maturity. Children do not thrive in isolation or loneliness. A child starts learning to bond at birth, and this intense thirst for attachment must be abundantly filled in the ensuing years. As this need is met, children receive a sense of belonging.

In the London Journal of Primary care, authors Winston and Chicot write, "Human babies are born very dependent on their parents. They undergo huge brain development, growth, and neuron pruning in the first two years of life. The brain development of infants (as well as their social, emotional, and cognitive development) depends on a loving bond or attachment relationship with a primary caregiver, usually a parent. There is increasing evidence from the fields of developmental psychology, neurobiology and animal epigenetic studies that neglect, parental inconsistency and a lack of love can lead to long-term mental health problems as well as to reduced overall potential and happiness."[144]

---

[143] Eccl 4:9-12. (NLT)

[144] Robert Winston and Rebecca Chicot. "The importance of early bonding on the long-term mental health and resilience of children," London Journal of Primary Care. (Feb. 24, 2016) https://www.ncbi.nlm.nih.gov/pmc/articles/PMC5330336/#idm139960142451152title

Bonding gives an inner cohesion to the whole BIOS of the learner. Bonding is the glue that helps form and holds the entire inner personality together. It provides a sense of emotional trust that things are generally all right and that the world is all right. Genuine bonding produces security, contentment, and a sense of acceptance. Lack of bonding creates inner pain, shreds the personality, and leads to destructive behavior. Studies have shown that children who have experienced a break in primary bonding are much more likely to get involved in illegal drugs and premarital intercourse. The counseling service Ambre Associates writes that childhood trauma leads to loneliness. Notably, this trauma includes,

- Early life attachment issues between a child and their parent or primary caregiver.
- Lack of unconditional love, including constant criticism.
- Neglect or abuse—physical, sexual or emotional; and/or,
- Loss of a parent or primary caregiver, whether through addiction, incarceration, abandonment, or death.[145]

This core human need never goes away.

Part of this deep yearning to belong is unique to man's spiritual nature and can only be fulfilled by knowing and experiencing direct fellowship (bonding/attachment) with God. This hunger to be joined (attached) in a real way with God is present no matter how secure or intimately we may have become attached to our mates and with others. King David wrote, "As the deer pants for streams of water, so I long for you, O God. I thirst for God, the living God. When can I come and stand before him? O God, you are my God; I earnestly search for you. My soul thirsts for you; my whole body longs for you in this parched and weary land where

[145] Denise K. Ambre, LCSW, Ambre Associates. (2020). https://www.ambre-associates.com/about-us.

there is no water. I have seen you in your sanctuary and gazed upon your power and glory. Your unfailing love is better to me than life itself; how I praise you. I reach out for you. I thirst for you as parched land thirsts for rain.[146]

Man's deepest longing to be joined to another in an intimate relationship is with God Himself. We were created to experience intimacy with God and to enjoy an ongoing relationship with Him. We were designed by God to find our security as we are joined to Him. He offers us a place of total acceptance and our joy is complete when we discover our extraordinary place of belonging in the love of God. In a sense then, all bonding relationships function to help us cultivate the capacity to bond in preparation for the eternal and permanent bonding when the community of believers (or bride of Christ) is wedded with the Lamb at His coming!

The intimate joys of relational bonding between husband and wife (Adam and Eve) and this first married couple together as one with God are revealed to us from the biblical record of primeval innocence in the first two holy institutions given to us by God—the wedding and the Sabbath.[147] Adam and Eve enjoyed the intimacy, closeness, and communion of the purest and most perfect kind between equals of the same class. Sabbath joined the first married couple in an intimate bond and spiritual intimacy with the living God in the highest and holiest kind of relationship between the Creator and His intelligent creatures.[148]

---

146 Ps. 42:1-2, 63:1-3, 143:6. (NLT)

147 Genesis 1 and 2.

148 In his commentary, Barnes beautifully expresses the depth and richness of both *God-given* institutions in the joining together (bonding) of husband and wife *in marriage* and of this first couple's bonding relationship with their creator *in Sabbath.* "Wedded union is the sum and type of every social tie. It gives rise and scope to all the nameless joys of home. It is the native field for the cultivation of all the social virtues. It provides for the due framing and checking of the overgrowth of interest in self, and for the gentle training and

Since God Himself puts such a premium on bonding, He built in automatic devices to help us. This unique process begins even before birth. Careful diet and exercise by a mother ensure the best physical environment for a child's development in the womb. The emotions of a pregnant mother affect the unborn's feelings. Pre-birth bonding has the potential to set the tone for life in a child before the child is even born. An unborn child begins to develop a fundamental worldview that the world is either a good place to be and feels accepted or feels alien to the world and not accepted. In unwanted pregnancies, some children sense rejection even before they are born. Mothers and fathers can foster early acceptance and begin building a loving relationship with their developing child by singing and talking to the unborn child as it is growing in the mother's womb. God has installed fascinating mechanisms from the moment of birth to facilitate deep and affectionate bonding between the newborn and his/her parents.

Dr. Donald M. Joy describes some of these in detail in his book, *Bonding*.

"There is a period (at birth) of heightened sensitivity to attachment. It seems to last for up to three hours following delivery...The

---

fostering of a growing interest in others. It unfolds the graces and charms of mutual love, and imparts to the susceptible heart all the peace and joy, all the light and fire, all the frankness and life of conscious and constant purity and good-will. Friendship, brotherly-kindness, and love are still hopeful and sacred names among mankind. Sabbath-keeping lifts the wedded pair, the brethren, the friends, the one-minded, up to communion (bonding) with God. The joy of achievement is a feeling common to God and man. The commemoration of the auspicious beginning of a holy and happy existence will live in man while memory lasts. The anticipation also of joyful repose after the end of a work well done will gild the future while hope survives. Thus, the idea of the Sabbath spans the whole of man's existence. History and prophecy commingle in the Sabbath's peaceful meditations, and both are linked with God. God IS: He is the Author of all being, and the Rewarder of them that diligently seek Him. This is the noble lesson of the Sabbath. Each seventh day is well spent in attending to the realization of these great thoughts." (from Barnes' Notes Gen. 2:25, http://www.Biblesoft.com)

visual acuity equips the newborn with search ability to locate the object to which to bond....The human mother tends to vocalize at the sight of her newborn, using sounds she does not usually use. These tend to be 'helium-like,' high-pitched speech to which the newborn is especially responsive."[149]

Dr. Joy continues, "Fathers are often advised to remove shirts so that both the warmth of the body and the magic of skin contact can communicate 'ownership' and affection to the infant...The unique aroma of the lanolin-laced lining of the placenta covers the newborn with a gentle skin treatment that has a unique odor. This odor appears to trigger 'encompassing' gesturing in the mother, sometimes almost involuntarily—enhancing the desire to hold, to cradle, and to embrace her baby."[150] What astounding and intricate provisions God has made to facilitate bonding at birth!

Bonding is a process that continues during every developmental phase of our children's lives. Good communication by parents with one another and their children is paramount to this continuing bonding/attachment process. John 1:1 states, "In the beginning was the Word, and the Word was with God, and the Word was God." One might say that God created communication and is the chief communicator.

Why?

God desires that we become bonded *to Him*! As explained in Hebrews, "Long ago God spoke many times and in many ways to our ancestors through the prophets. But now in these final days, he has spoken to us through his Son. So, we must listen very carefully to the truth we have heard, or we may drift away from it. The message God delivered through angels has always proved true, and the people were punished for every violation of the law and every act of disobedience. What makes us think that we can escape if

---

[149] Dr. Donald M. Joy, *Bonding*. (Nappanee, IN: Evangel, 1987). 114-115.

[150] Ibid. 115.

we are indifferent to this great salvation that was announced by the Lord Jesus himself? It was passed on to us by those who heard him speak, and God verified the message by signs and wonders and various miracles and by giving gifts of the Holy Spirit whenever he chose to do so."[151] As our heavenly father, God has, is, and continues to be wholly involved with us as His children as an excellent communicator.

Children's minds and hearts are reservoirs for our words. They ask hundreds of thousands of questions during the first few years of life. Each question allows parents the opportunity to respond in truth and love, thereby affirming the importance of our children, and fostering curiosity and a genuine love of learning. At this stage of life, children are assimilating rules of grammar, building a worldview of life, and learning to understand and speak a language—without any formal education. And they do it all without one report card. How we handle our verbal relationships with our children during the early years, to a great extent builds, develops, and begins to establish the parameters of all future learning experiences. Taking time to talk and read often to these precious gifts from God does more to determine future academic success than any subsequent formal learning program or curriculum.

Bonding also is facilitated by allowing our children freedom of expression. Our home environments need to encourage freedom for our children's expression of *their* feelings, thoughts, and ideas. Allowing our children to be real is not the same as being permissive. Established guidelines can be contested without being broken by children. Moments of open dialog about the purpose of rules and behavior can promote deeper bonding. Being authentic in our conversations with our children on difficult topics holds the potential for becoming markers on the pathway to fruitfulness in relationships and achievement. How we openly handle

[151] Hebrews 1:1-2, 2:1-4. (NLT)

disagreements with our children and spouses helps to teach respectful problem resolution. This is a valuable lifelong skill that can be honed at home.

Our primary family guideline has always been to encourage honest and truthful communication. By keeping honest thoughts and real feelings in the open, accurate biblical responses are possible. *Real relationships* facilitate genuine bonding.

During life, we form some of our closest bonds with others through adversity. The same is true in the family setting. How we handle difficult times together as a family can produce deep relationships that do not occur during "good" times. Adversity can be met head-on with mutual support. Hanging out together brings insight for solving problems when the time is right. Suggestions for overcoming daily challenges sometimes come from the least expected person. God often speaks to us through our children in revealing solutions to our dilemmas. Openness to finding the most favorable response to life's difficult situations together develops respect for all family members. The result strengthens personal family bonds.

In retrospect, we have discovered that the best way to fight debilitating peer pressure is by meeting the needs of our children during their first few years of life at home. Life offers a multitude of opportunities to spend time together through every developmental stage of our children's growth cycle. Our families are a micro-community. Mutual support of one another through the changing interests and activities of our children as they grow meets their needs and sustains this healthy bonding process.

To accomplish this goal, there is a cost to our self-life as parents. Our being there for basketball games, theatre performances, ballet lessons and recitals, and a host of other classroom and extracurricular projects all take time. But real interest and involvement produce genuine bonds that are a strong deterrent to the overwhelming onslaught of negative peer pressure and influence that our children will encounter.

Family traditions also build memories and strengthen bonds that will last a lifetime. Each family is unique in developing its traditions. One of our family's favorite times consists of making our famous brewers' yeast popcorn and enjoying a movie that all five of us have finally agreed was worth watching. This decision is usually reached only after much haggling over each of our personal preferences. But more than watching the movie itself, the heart of this fun is the joy of just being together.

The same goes for meals (at home or out) that provide multiple opportunities to allow discovery, bonding, and relationships to grow deeply with one another. Jokes and pranks add to the spice of family life. We were out eating at one of our favorite restaurants when I had the waitress deliver my son's dessert to our table. He was away at the restroom. Before he left the table, he had ordered cheesecake, from a display dessert tray that had foam rubber replicas of all the desserts. I asked the waitress to bring the foam rubber cheesecake to the place where he was sitting. He caught on to what I had done only after a few repeated attempts to carve off a piece of his cheesecake with his fork. We still laugh about that incident to this day.

Mealtime affords one of the best opportunities for all kinds of interaction to occur. But in our society moving at a breakneck pace, these times must be carved out and protected. If not, they can vanish, and that is a significant loss for everyone. I love sitting at a table surrounded by our children and guests. There is something deeply satisfying about such relationships that our heavenly Father has given us for our enjoyment. There is a great enjoyment to be found around the table in affectionate bonding relationships with our children and with others.[152]

There are many other creative ways to build memories and bonds. Today there is an arsenal of electronic equipment including smartphones to capture moments that can be reviewed and enjoyed many times over. I weathered the complaints of Andrew, Elizabeth, and Jonathan with my antics in using my cameras (I'm a photographer) to preserve photographs and videos of many moments during our family events and excursions. Now our three adult children are doing the same. Our library of memories continues to grow. Occasionally at family gatherings, we break some of these out. We see the good, bad, and the ugly. And we see all the moments that we have cherished together through the years. Now I am getting video shorts on my smartphone, and show them to one of my grandsons as he sits on my lap. Another bonding moment!

Finally, one of the most vital areas for real bonding comes from sharing a purpose or mission. The prayerful desire to see God's kingdom ultimately blossom into its full glory has motivated Gretchen and me through our married life. It still does. It is an incredible joy to see our children fully engaged in knowing God, seeking to do His will, obeying His commandments, and connecting with others in outreach as we all continue to press on toward the same goal. The ultimate bonding we can share with our family members is to be bonded together with God and His purposes as His children. Such a bond will never be broken. Bonding with God's mission and purpose is one of the most profound

---

152 Psalm 122 verse 3 says, "Jerusalem is a well-built city, knit together as a single unit." (NLT) In reference to Jerusalem as the city of God's dwelling place, this reference really means that this is a place where fellowship is complete! What a wonderful picture. As a microcity of God's habitation, our families offer us a refuge and place where our fellowship (relationships) can be complete. To put it another way, our hearts and spirits can be so full, that there will not be a need to look elsewhere for any additional fulfillment. What a provision God has made for His children *while living here on earth*!

blessings we can pass on to our children as they receive the inheritance of our hearts. This comes from God.

Love and deep bonding (attachment) are the first two relational foundations for developing the optimum BIOS in our children. These relational foundations become the basis and motivating force that provide the two subsequent relational foundations in the development of our children's BIOS. The second two of these four building blocks, leadership/discipline, and equipping/mentoring are explored more fully in the following chapter.

Together, these four relational foundations impart a complete functioning relational BIOS, which becomes the core for genuine wholehearted learning for our children throughout life.

Chapter 11

# Discipline

## Relational Foundations

As discussed in the previous chapter, love and bond/attachment are the first two relational foundations for developing our children's BIOS. Real love is the motivating force for true biblical learning. Love, along with a strong bond, provides the proper environment for establishing the next two relational foundations for wholehearted learning. The remaining two foundations, *discipline* and *mentoring*, are two joint aspects of wholehearted training.

It may be helpful at this point to visualize how all four relational foundations relate to each other before exploring the remaining two. Notice in the following diagram that love is not only one of the foundations but undergirds the whole foundational structure. Solid biblical love is the bedrock for attachment, discipline, and instruction. The presence of genuine love also provides the ability and guiding principles for the proper application of discipline and instruction throughout the entire process of biblical learning for us as parents.

## The Four *Relational* Foundations

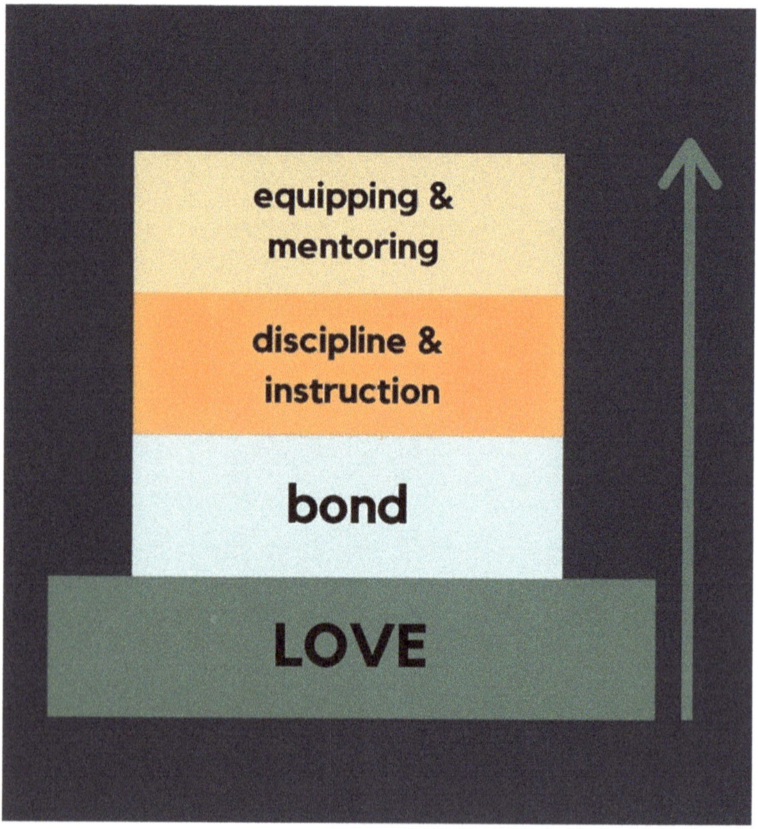


***Love is the foundation and motivating force***

The four relational building blocks that we as parents must provide are *love, bonding, discipline,* and *mentoring*. In biblical learning, all four relational foundations are interconnected and interrelated. They are inseparable. Biblical training is the result of the proper application of discipline and instruction throughout the learning process. Equipping or mentoring are two other terms that describe instruction, especially after the first few years of life. All four relational foundations will be present in authentic biblical learning because real biblical learning is wholehearted learning, which forms character, alters behavior, and builds life skills and learning achievement.

Outstanding public accomplishments and performances of great athletes and musicians are the outcomes of the private commitment to the discipline of these individuals. Discipline is a necessary ingredient that must be present to become proficient in anything. This same principle applies, *especially* in biblical learning. In 1 Timothy 4:7, Paul writes to one of his younger disciples, "... Spend your time and energy in training yourself for spiritual fitness. Physical exercise has some value, but spiritual exercise is much more important, for it promises a reward in both this life and the next." (NLT)

The goal of wholehearted learning is the transformation of one's nature to share the inward likeness of Christ.[153] The purpose of external discipline is to lead us into the experience of internal control through the indwelling presence of the Holy Spirit and grace of God. Discipline is not opposed to grace. Abundant grace produces outstanding discipline. Paul writes, "But whatever I am now, it is all because God poured out his special favor on me—and not without results. For I have worked harder than all the other apostles, yet it was not I but God who was working through me *by his grace*."[154] [emphasis added] This is the beauty and essence of wholehearted learning. Through an intimate relationship with Jesus, it is possible to live within the borders of God's loving instructions. Jesus, our example, who was the Living Word kept the commandments! He gives us, as His children, the ability to live within the blessed parameters of His law. Keeping His

---

153 This is the process of having the laws of God written on our hearts by the Holy Spirit. See Jer. 31:31-33.

154 1 Cor. 15:10. (NLT)

commandments preserves our life, and develops the highest potentials for growth and achievement.

Disciplining our children in the early years is one of the most challenging and confusing functions we must fulfill to lead our children along the pathway to emotional and spiritual wholeness and productive achievement in learning and lifestyle. Over the last several years, there has been an explosion of information on child discipline. Unfortunately, much of it is false and unverifiable. God's word is the most accurate and reliable source of information on child discipline and provides beneficial, valid results when properly applied. The soundness of biblical principles of discipline (training/control) has mostly been lost through ignorance. Rebellious parents have consciously rejected God and His loving instructions resulting in damage to their parenting.

Solomon directly addresses this issue in Proverbs by saying, "If you refuse to discipline your children, it proves you don't love them; if you love your children, you will be prompt to discipline them."[155] The outcome of loving discipline is described in Proverbs 29:17-18, "Discipline your children, and they will give you happiness and peace of mind. When people do not accept divine guidance, they run wild. But whoever obeys the law is happy." What rare commodities have become happiness and peace of mind for parents regarding their children today. Yet these are the very outcomes that are the result of applying loving discipline during our children's early years. This training process seems painful at the time but produces joy for parents as children move into early adulthood.

The predisposition to corrupt morals and behavior within all of us makes appropriate discipline for children inevitable. Hebrews 12:6-8 states, "For the Lord disciplines those he loves, and he punishes those he accepts as his children. As you endure this divine discipline, remember that God is treating you as his children.

[155] Prov. 13:24. (NLT)

Whoever heard of a child who was never disciplined? If God does not discipline you as he does all of his children, it means that you are illegitimate and are not his children after all." Biblical discipline is a process that helps redirect the natural tendency to be foolish into reshaping character filled with wisdom. The seeds of proper training sewn by parents into the lives of children return an eventual harvest of blessing, happiness, and peace of mind. If children are not disciplined, they will become an instrument of sorrow to their parents. The outcomes of the choice parents exercise in disciplining their children are shown below.

**the proper application of discipline leads to happiness and peace of mind**

- A wise child brings joy to a father. Prov. 10:1
- The father of godly children has cause for joy. What a pleasure it is to have wise children. So, give your parents joy! May she who gave you birth be happy. Prov. 23:24-25
- Discipline your children, and they will give you happiness and peace of mind. When people do not accept divine guidance, they run wild. But whoever obeys the law is happy. Prov. 29:17-18

## discipline withheld leads to sadness and pain

- A foolish child brings grief to a mother. Prov. 10:1
- It is painful to be the parent of a fool; there is no joy for the father of a rebel. Prov. 17:21
- To discipline and reprimand a child produces wisdom, but a mother is disgraced by an undisciplined child. Prov. 29:15

God, as our loving heavenly Father, has given parents the provision of His truth for applying relational discipline (parent to child) so that our lives ultimately will be full of joy rather than pain and sorrow as our children grow into adulthood. It is our responsibility to seek this truth and then to apply it in the training of our children. Our goal as parents is to serve God as our children's mentors so they reach the purpose which God has created them to fulfill. In this process, we become co-laborers with God.

Biblical training is a process that *disciplines* (controls and restrains) our children from merely following the natural inclination to sin (miss God's mark) and to give *instruction* that will teach our children the pathway of life. Proverbs 22:6, says, "Teach your children to choose the right path, and when they are older, they will remain upon it." Notice what this verse is saying. God is not saying we are to force our children into the right path. He is giving us the commandment as parents *to teach* our children in such a manner that they *will choose* the right way. God's love in us and our love for our children should permeate the atmosphere in which we discipline and instruct our children. As our children experience our love and God's love for them during the whole process of discipline and instruction, they will desire to choose the right path.

One historical picture that God carefully recorded in His relationship with Israel illustrates the pattern of discipline that applies to training our children. External control leads to the development of internal control. The law (external control) was given to Israel to preserve and protect them until the coming of the Messiah. His coming, death, resurrection, and the subsequent gift of the Holy Spirit (internal control) made possible the fulfillment and purpose for His people as prophesied by the prophet Jeremiah, "But this is the new covenant I will make with the people of Israel on that day," says the LORD. "I will put my laws in their minds, and I will write them on their hearts. I will be their God, and they will be my people."[156] As discussed earlier,[157] the engrafting of God's loving instructions in our hearts by the indwelling presence of the Holy Spirit produces ultimate wholeness and self-control. God intended for man to live from the inside out. Quality of life, the fullness of joy, and fruitful achievement are gifts given for our advantage as we are guided by God's internal compass (His laws). And the very power of God in us as we receive the gift of the Holy Spirit gives us the ability to keep them.

I attended grade school in Denver, Colorado. We had an extensive playground area. Streets bordered three sides of the playground, one of which was a bustling thoroughfare. Fortunately, the playground was surrounded by a high chainlink fence that protected

---

[156] Jer. 31:33. (NLT)

[157] Please see Chapter 2, footnote 28 for a complete description of peace (*shalom*).

us from inadvertently running out into the streets while playing. Safe and secure, we enjoyed our kickball games immensely. Had the barriers been removed, we would have been afraid to play with such unhindered abandon. Although the fence had the appearance of a restriction, it was a loving boundary that gave us security and freedom to play without being harmed. Through applied discipline, parents provide the *relational boundaries* that children need to feel secure and to grow to maximum potential without hindrances.

Until children are old enough to grasp verbal instruction (which leads to internal control), parents are God's gift to their children to provide them with the external controlling boundaries (through discipline), which will keep them safe from harm and help them grow into adulthood. Parents receive this delegated authority from God.[158] By providing a loving disciplined environment, parents help their children develop emotional security, which enhances all later learning experiences. Control must be established *before* genuine instruction is possible. The only commandment[159] given to children by God while they are under the

---

[158] In Exod. 21:15,17, flagrant disrespect of parental authority was actually punishable by death! This tragic penalty was not given because God is cruel. As an external control, this penalty served as a stern warning to all of Israel that if the governmental structure of the home was undermined that the destruction and ultimate extinction of all of Israel would follow. Rebellion against God's governmental structure in the home would place the whole culture at risk. The *intent* of God behind this penalty is the same as the intent behind all of the commandments of God—to preserve *life*! See also, Deut. 21:18-21, 27:16, and Prov. 30:17. In all these references, contempt, disrespect, or mocking of one's parents would bring a curse upon the children. *Suffering and pain* for children *and* parents are the inevitable consequences of ignoring or rebelling against His governmental structure in the home. In Matthew 15:4, Jesus rebukes the *adult* leaders (scribes and Pharisees) for their failure to honor their parents by substituting their own traditions in order escape this law of God which required that they *continue to honor their parents* by helping to take care of their needs in later life.

[159] "Children, obey your parents because you belong to the Lord, for this is the right thing to do." Eph 6:1. Col. 3:20 states, "You children must always obey

authority of their parents is designed to develop this relational control between parent and child.

Obedience is a profoundly simple governmental principle. This first principle must be learned and learned well. It is the foundation for all governmental principles that will later be applied in the classroom and all legitimate governmental structures. Everyone must learn to live lawfully within the governmental structures of their respective society and culture. The maintenance of every nation is affected by the proper understanding of government and lawful behavior.[160]

In God's design, the home is the preeminent learning institution for establishing obedience, discipline, and proper government. Parents are God's delegated authority to accomplish this purpose. From the beginning, the responsibility for the training of children has belonged to a child's own father and mother. Obedience is an attitude of heart and behavior that is forged and learned by children from their parents in the crucible of the home. Unfortunately, this responsibility is often abdicated by the parents to their church, schools, and governmental agencies. Some of these institutions are eager to assume the role forfeited by parents. Unfortunately, these attempts to remediate the failure of this crucial role of parents, are costly and inadequate. Most are complete failures. Any program or institution which intentionally or unintentionally undermines the role of the parents in this crucial role rather than supporting it is shortsighted and ultimately structurally flawed.

God's commandment for children to be raised in the "nurture and admonition of the Lord" as found in Deut. 6:6-7[161] and reit-

---

your parents, for this is what pleases the Lord.

[160] God has ordained governmental structures for the orderly maintenance of all societies and cultures. See Romans 13:1-10.

[161] Please review Chapter 4 where this original mandate for instructing one's own children was first given to parents by God.

erated in Ephesians 6:4 is given to parents. By combining various translations of Ephesians 6:4 the phrase "nurture and admonition of the Lord" can be rendered as follows: *Don't make your children angry by the way you treat them. Rather, bring them up with the discipline and instruction approved by the Lord.*

First, note that this is the kind of discipline which is approved by the Lord. How often do we purchase something that needs to be assembled before use? In our excitement, we hurriedly attempt to put all the pieces together only to realize we have left something out. Or we encounter pieces we cannot fit together or end up with "extras." In frustration and exasperation, we break down and get out the owner's manual. How much easier the whole process would have been if only we had started with the owner's manual in the first place. In child discipline, why not begin with the owner's manual (God's instructions)? Stephanie Hanuck who has been working as a Pre-K teacher for the last eight years in various states writes, "It's time for parents to take back the reins at home and begin teaching their children right from wrong before they reach the classroom."[162]

Establishing the right kind of discipline is one of the most critical components in assembling our children's BIOS. With our proper application of discipline and training, our children will grow up functioning beautifully. We will have Pentium children

---

[162] Hanuck, Stephanie. (January 6, 2020). *Opinion: What Schools Are Getting Wrong on Discipline. We are Teachers.* https://www.weareteachers.com/school-discipline-failures. "It has to be said—the line between parent and child has become increasingly blurry over the last few decades. More and more, we see children who are coming to school with terrible manners, selfish attitudes and inappropriate social behaviors. When students don't learn to behave appropriately at home, those behaviors transfer into the school setting. In Dr. Leonard Sax's "The Collapse of Parenting", he talks about the "transfer of authority from parents to kids" as a key player in children's changing behaviors (Italie, 2016). Children who dictate what's for dinner, when bedtime is, and how much time they get to play on the computer will not be successful at school or in the real world."

(fully functioning children). Our culture and society want Pentium children without ever installing a proper BIOS, but discipline cannot be overlooked or ignored. It is one of the essential foundations needed to form our children's BIOS.

Nurture means training by *disciplinary correction.* Disciplinary correction includes *chastisement* through which early instruction is accomplished. Chastise comes from the Hebrew word *yacar*, whose primitive root means to instruct literally *with blows* or figuratively *with words*. Additional meanings include punish, reform, reprove, and teach. Chastisement (or discipline) has as its goal the *saving of the mind.* Biblical training invites and directs our children to the soundness of mind or self-control. The word *admonition* means calling attention to by mild rebuke or warning. *Yacar* is the form of discipline given by God to parents for their children's ultimate well-being.

Proverbs 19:18 says, "Discipline (chasten) your children while there is hope. If you don't, you will ruin their lives." The implication here is that children should be disciplined at the dawn of their lives. It is so easy to think that in due time we will correct our children. But as soon as a corrupt disposition appears, immediate discipline will check further growth before a rebellious attitude or misbehavior takes root and hardens into a habit. Pulling up weeds early in a garden is accomplished more quickly than putting off the necessary labor until the weeds have firmly rooted. Deeply rooted habits, like weeds in a garden, become much more difficult to root out the longer they are allowed to grow.

Biblical discipline was never intended to be frustrating for either parent or child. God's purpose of correctly applied discipline is to bring the necessary correction into children's lives to turn foolishness into wisdom and failure into fulfillment. These principles must be applied in an age-relevant manner to be effective and useful. It is beyond the scope of this writing to map out particular disciplinary guidelines for each developmental growth phase. There are many excellent resources available to provide help in this area.[163] Consequently, I will share just a glimpse of discipline methods Gretchen and I used with our children. In the earliest years when our children misbehaved—before they had developed real cognitive abilities—discipline was accomplished using physical means such as a wooden spoon.[164] As our children grew in age and understanding, one most effective means of discipline we found was to restrict them from engaging in one of their favorite pastimes such as playing video games.

At an early age, a child's sinful nature (each child is born with one[165]) seeks to enslave him through a constant pull to fulfill his strong desires. Left to himself, a child becomes self-centered. Without any mechanisms of self-control developed, children have a desperate need for a parent's help in controlling (disciplining) their sinful nature. Solomon writes, "The rod and reproof give wisdom, but a child who gets his way brings shame to his mother."[166]

A story in the old testament describes the terrible judgment that came to Eli, the high priest who had served all of Israel as their judge for forty years but failed to fulfill his God-given mandate to discipline his children, Hophni and Phinehas. The prophet Samuel spoke the following words to Eli. "I will carry out against Eli everything I spoke against his family—from beginning to end. For I told him that I would judge his family forever because of

---

163 James Dobson *Dare To Discipline*. (Wheaton, IL: Tyndale House, 1970).

164 See footnote 172, Chapter 12.

165 Ps. 51:5 records King David's assessment of his condition at birth and *even at conception*. "For I was born a sinner—yes, from the moment my mother conceived me." Man's pride makes the acknowledge of his true condition before God very difficult. Apart from the revelation of God concerning the human condition, parents do not want to acknowledge that their innocent newborn has any predisposition to sin.

166 Prov. 29:15. (NAS)

the sin he knew about; *his sons made themselves contemptible*, and *he failed to restrain (discipline) them*."[167] (Italics mine)

Subsequently, due to Eli's failure to discipline his two sons, Eli lost his life and both his sons were killed in battle. The wife of Phinehas died in childbirth. Not only did this tragedy come upon Eli's household but also upon an entire nation. In two days, 34,004 died, and the presence of God was removed from a whole nation.

All this happened because Eli, the high priest, failed as a parent to discipline his two sons whose unrestrained corrupt human nature had made them contemptible.

Why do children need to be disciplined?

It is because of the malignancy of unrestrained (uncontrolled) corrupt human nature as so vividly illustrated in the lives of Hophni and Phinehas. Their brutality and lust were known to everyone in their community.

Numerous shootings carried out by troubled individuals today are all stark reminders of this truth. In the early years of life, children desperately need the help of their parents in restraining the natural tendency toward unlawful and destructive behavior either to themselves or others. Understanding and applying God's design for authority, obedience, and discipline in the home are life and death issues.

Thankfully, God has provided clear guidelines and effective tools to help parents succeed in disciplining children. Parental authority is a delegated authority that comes from God, as stated previously. It is imperative that, as parents, we first submit ourselves to the government of God in our own lives. Parents who have first brought their own lives under obedience to God through a relationship with Him will be equipped to apply the necessary discipline in their children's lives in love and fairness.

---

[167] 1 Sam. 3:12-13. (NIV) Please see 1 Samuel chapters 1 through 4 for this gruesome story of failure.

Parents are the first personal representatives of *who God is* to their children. What a remarkable call this is for us! How careful we need to be in showing the nature of God to our children by how we discipline them. God gives us the power to control our children. This encompasses the authority to administer justice, to punish for disobedience, and to reward for obedience. Included with this authority is a grant by God Himself, to use force if necessary, to resolve inevitable conflicts that occur when a child disobeys by misbehavior or when a child rebels against being controlled. It must be pointed out that biblical discipline never was intended to be arbitrary or authoritarian. Correct discipline for a child from a parent is deeper than just "being in charge." Real discipline/training has the benefit of a child as its goal, not any self-gratifying or capricious behavior on the part of a parent at the expense of a child.

The proper use of authority establishes obedience in children. Obedience is demonstrated when a child consistently does what he has been told, even if it is in contradiction to his own will or desire for the moment. This kind of obedience to parents' authority helps children develop respect for their parents, which in turn causes children to be receptive to their parents' verbal instruction (mentoring). Respect is a prerequisite for receiving the full benefit of learning from verbal instruction between parent and child. As children develop emotionally and mature mentally, this respect is transferred to others in authority and other teachers outside the home. Respect is one of the most vital ingredients necessary in the learning process.

Parents who fulfill God's mandate to bring their children up "in the discipline and instruction approved by the Lord"[168] help their children fulfill the commandment given to them as children, to

---

[168] Eph. 6:4.

obey and honor their parents.[169] Our children's capacities to learn, and the application of this learning to their personal lives—and for the benefit of others—to a large extent will be determined by how well we do in fulfilling our mandate.

Disciplining our children is a process we learn as parents. Our unseasoned mistakes and failures will not derail the outcome. As we follow God's guidelines and utilize His methods for disciplining and instructing our children, we will know the eventual peace and joy that is promised.

The nature of godly discipline is wonderfully portrayed in David's description of a good shepherd. God's relationship with his children is characterized by the same protective, caring relationship that a shepherd has with his sheep. As undershepherds with God, we receive the ability to shepherd our children as He does His children. Children know they are loved when they experience this kind of discipline. Such discipline provides security and comfort, which they desire. I have taken the liberty to insert a few additional words in italics below to illustrate this point. David writes,[170]

"The LORD (*my parents are*) is my shepherd. I have everything I need. He lets (*they let*) me rest in green meadows. He leads (*they lead*) me beside peaceful streams. He renews (*they help me renew*) my strength. He guides (*my parents' guide*) me along right paths, bringing honor to his name. Even when I walk through the dark valley of death, I will not be afraid, for you are close beside me. Your rod and your staff protect and comfort me. You prepare a

---

169 Eph. 6:1-2.

170 Ps. 23:1-6. I have added the words in italics to emphasize the total attitude, atmosphere, and actions that godly parents will exhibit as they nurture and discipline their children. Notice that the proper use of the rod and staff is a *comfort* to the sheep, not a threat. Parents are able to love this way because they *already* know and are experiencing this kind of love from God for themselves through their relationship with Him.

feast for me in the presence of my enemies. You welcome me as a guest, anointing my head with oil. My cup overflows with blessings. Surely your goodness and unfailing love will pursue me all the days of my life, and I will live in the house of the LORD forever."

As parents, the discipline and instruction of our children is a function we fulfill in the context of being good shepherds to our children. Parenting with a shepherd's heart sets the tone for the nurturing and discipline of our children. All we do to discipline our children is because we tenderly love and care for them, as good shepherds do for the sheep under their care.

Administering discipline is often inconvenient (children seldom misbehave at an opportune moment in our schedules) and embarrassing (when we are with others). But a good shepherd will lay down his own life (self-life) for the benefit of his sheep. This means that immediate and effective discipline will be more important to us than our convenience or "saving face" with our friends when our children's behavior needs correcting.

Self-discipline and an accurate inner moral compass are essential elements in our children's internal BIOS. Our primary goal as parents in the process of disciplining our children is to help our children develop their internal control and guidance (direction) system for life. To reach this goal, it is helpful to visualize this process in three training/instructional phases (time frames). God has given us specific instructions and tools to help us accomplish this goal. As our children progress from immaturity to maturity and from the need for external control to internal self-control the choice of appropriate forms of discipline will mature as well.

Chapter 12

# The Three Phases of Discipline

## Relational Foundations

**The** three primary phases of discipline and instruction may be visualized along a timeline as follows.

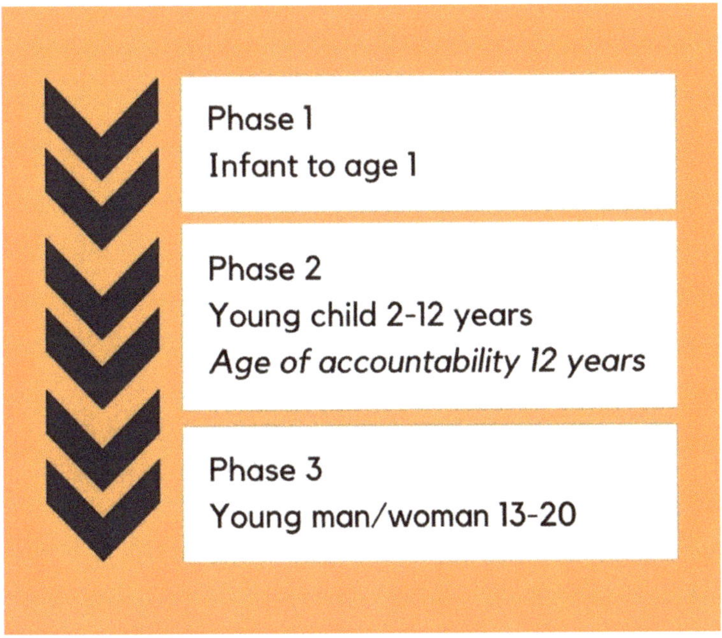


As our children grow, they are on a constant pilgrimage through these three phases toward maturity. Honor and respect for one's parents as well as obedience to them and God are the prerequisites and foundation for acquiring biblical learning. Discipline aims to lead our children into the development of self-control (internal control). Directing our children to the standards that will help them fully develop their moral compass helps to impart genuine respect for authority. That kind of respect enables our children's maximum ability to receive later instruction. Such respect will also allow our children to fully accept the instructional equipping that will properly fit them for living and the fulfillment of God's call for their own lives as they mature and grow into adulthood.

Once again, God's word gives explicit instruction to parents concerning His guidelines for helping us accomplish these goals. Correctly and consistently applied, these God-given disciplinary guidelines will produce the fruit we are seeking for our children's ultimate well-being and achievement.

As these guidelines are now considered, great care must be exercised in understanding the proper means and purpose for applying each of these three phases.

## Phase One

When Gretchen and I lived in the Pink Flamingo trailer in northern Wisconsin, we carried our water from a nearby hand pump, and our only source of heat to stay warm during the long winters was a wood-burning Ashley stove. It took a lot of hardwood and an extremely hot fire to help dispel the cold encroachment through the three-inch walls in subzero temperatures. Occasionally the outer liner of our stove would start glowing. It had become red hot.

Andrew was a toddler during that time. In our concern for his safety, the first two words he needed to grasp the meaning of were "no" and "hot." One day he began heading right past my "no" to explore the "hot" stove. Curiosity and a challenge to parental authority come early in life. I intervened, grabbed Andrew, reached for a small stick (rod), and gave Andrew his first spanking.

I had never done anything more difficult in my life as a parent than to apply physical discipline to our firstborn, whom Gretchen and I both loved deeply. I did not in any way want to have to inflict any physical pain on our son.[171] It just didn't seem right or loving. But at that moment, I had to act for our son's ultimate well-being. He had to learn that "no" meant "no." The swift physical action and momentary pain formed a connection to the word "no" that registered deeply in Andrew's internal BIOS and affected all his future behavior. "No" had now become a certain external restraint that saved Andrew from ever having to experience the excruciating pain he would have suffered had he laid his hands against a red-hot wood stove.

That action, on my part, welded a new bond between Andrew and me. At the deepest level, there was a clear line of authority established, which immediately became a place of security and safety for Andrew. He could count on me to act on my word. I had not disciplined Andrew because I was mad at him. I had taken action to teach Andrew the meaning of the word "no" for his benefit, in the language he could understand at that exceedingly early age.

Solomon learned something significant from his father, King David. In Proverbs 13:24, he writes the following, "He who spares the rod hates his son, but he who loves him is careful to discipline him." (NIV) If necessary, the proper use of a rod is one of the

---

[171] It is a natural feeling for us as parents not to want to hurt our children. This is our natural instinct. To help us overcome this God has given us His word in order to do what is best for our children. Proverbs 23, verses 13-14 says, "Don't fail to correct your children. They won't die if you spank them. Physical discipline may well save them from death." See also: 2 Sam. 7:14, Prov. 13:24, Prov. 19:18, Prov. 22:15, Prov. 23:13-14, Prov. 29:15, and Heb. 12:6-7. All these references show the *need for* and the *positive results* of the proper use of the rod as an instrument of correction.

first tools given by God to parents for disciplining children. It is a physical expression of our love, which we may need to use for our children's good.

What is a rod?

A shepherd's rod or staff has multiple functions. A rod is a mark or symbol of authority. Within the realm of authority for the care of his sheep, the shepherd uses his rod for guidance, correction, and protection of his sheep. In ancient times, sheep would pass under a shepherd's rod as he counted each of his sheep. Walking under the shepherd's rod was symbolic of coming under the shepherd's total care.

A rod[172] is God's prescribed instrument for the chastisement of children by parents. A rod is a narrow stick that will produce a sting and will give the same results used by either a mother or father.

God padded buttocks for a reason. Besides being portable cushions, they are also excellent receptors. They were fashioned to transmit a direct and instantaneous message to the brain when struck by a rod. The most sensitive layer of skin in a child's hindquarters is close to the surface where the nerve endings are located. The objective of chastisement is not to beat a child into submission using brute force or to hurt the child. The pain received from a rod is more humbling to a child than harmful. Any object used that causes more than surface pain could injure a child and produce

---

172 The rod is a thin wooden stick. The size will vary depending upon the age of a child, from a small branch to a more substantial stick like a dowel rod. It can cause stripes and yet will not do any permanent damage even if used strenuously. Some children may scream *as if* they are dying when the rod is being used. Children's response to correction has not changed since ancient times, nor will they "die" when being corrected. Solomon noted this truth in Prov. 23:13:14 by writing, "Don't fail to correct your children. They won't die if you spank them. Physical discipline may well save them from death. See also 2 Sam 7:14 and Heb. 12:6.

guilt in a parent, neither of which are the desired outcomes of biblical correction.

Chastisement is the proper use of the rod when a child is disobedient in willful rejection of parental authority. For the child's ultimate well-being a rebellious attitude must be swiftly and decisively addressed.

As a symbol of parental authority, a rod is a neutral object, unlike the hand, which is a part of our person and should represent protection, comfort, and beckoning. When the rod is appropriately used, the child's complete attention is focused on the instrument of pain, rather than on the person using it. A child does not identify a rod with anything other than his rebellion and the pain that results from his defiance of authority. After the use of the rod, our arms and hands hold and comfort our children, as they feel our love, acceptance, and forgiveness.

Proper use of the rod in God's design is a symbol of parents' God-given authority. Early in this process of discipline, the child should learn from his parents that they are as willing to obey God's word as they expect their children to follow theirs. Once children become old enough to grasp verbal explanations for the reasons they have been corrected, the moments immediately following such correction becomes the most receptive times children exhibit in really learning new habits, self-control, and renewed thinking for similar circumstances in the future.

Andrew's discipline was a learning experience for me too. I had been set free from my feelings of never wanting to discipline any of our children physically. I realized in a profound way that I had expressed a genuine love for him by my actions. Andrew comprehended the meaning of the word "no" at a level in which no verbal explanation could have penetrated at that age. From then on, he would circle the stove at a safe distance. Andrew then began using the word "hot," even though there was yet no meaning to that word in his mental development. "No" had become a boundary that would keep him safe until he could later understand the verbal meaning of the word "hot."

How relevant is this to the educational process?

Discipline is *the* prerequisite to learning. As I mentioned before, educators in every public and private sector cite discipline/control as their number one problem.[173] If students will not listen and do not understand the meaning of the word "no," which is a Phase One learning experience, how can a teacher ever move beyond establishing discipline to teaching a curriculum? Parents' failure to discipline their children inevitably forces this responsibility on others outside the home. This failure undermines the gifts, talents, and abundant resources of teachers who end up spending most of their time struggling with classroom discipline rather than teaching. There are no winners. In despair, seasoned professional educators are leaving the classroom jungles in search of new professions that will not destroy them. Many are giving up on what has become a hopeless environment for instruction and learning.

From Wisconsin, we moved to Arkansas. Elizabeth and Jonathan were born in our new place. What a change! It felt like we had moved from Siberia to the Tropics. We had enough space for me to garden and raise sheep. Each year, I couldn't wait until springtime.

Every morning I would walk up the hill just above our home to see if our pregnant ewes had lambed yet. I loved picking up the wobble-kneed, black-faced baby lambs the day they were born and carrying them into our house to show Andrew, Elizabeth, and Jonathan.

Day after day, as I fed, wormed, and sheared our sheep, I would talk to them. They recognized my voice. It was interesting to watch their response to strangers. They would scatter or not even bother

---

[173] See footnote 162, Chapter 11.

to lift their heads when a stranger would approach and talk to them. But they knew me and recognized my voice.

On a daily check, I found one of our sheep outside the fence. A neighbor's dog had ripped open the thin skin beneath the thick wool. I could see the insides of this ewe beneath the tears. We hurried as quickly as we could to a local veterinarian. After multiple stitches and a drainage tube was inserted, we headed home in hopes that healing would mend these extensive wounds and that our sheep would survive. With tender loving care, thankfully this ewe pulled through.

I once heard a story of a shepherd who had an unruly and wayward lamb who bounded endlessly outside of safety into dangerous areas without ever heeding the voice of the shepherd. Fearing the loss of this lamb, the shepherd broke one of its legs. The shepherd then carried the lamb on his shoulders and spoke to it continuously as the leg was healing. In the process, the lamb came to know and understand the shepherd's voice. The shepherd's painful yet loving action had spared the destruction of this lamb by wolves, in which territory it had been recklessly wandering.

In the same way, children must learn to obey for their safety. They must learn to trust and obey their parents' words. Proper use of the rod accomplishes this purpose and prepares children to learn from the verbal instruction of their parents. Parents' words then become a standard for behavior for children and serve as guidelines for further growth toward maturity.

During Phase One, training and teaching restraint and obedience are most effectively learned by immediate and appropriate use of the rod when children refuse (attitude) or fail to obey (behavior) the parent's voice. Once honor and respect, as well as the governmental right to rule (parental authority), is established, early Phase Two learning is the time in which verbal instructions are used to teach standards that are rooted in God's loving instructions and guidance. During this time, punishment trains and teaches children the consequences and need for restitution when known rules have been broken.

## *Phase Two*

Phase Two is the essential time for establishing and teaching standards. Standards are rules to be kept. Every home will develop its unique standards of behavior. Whatever these standards are, they must be designed for the child's well-being and in harmony with God's word and His rules. As children grow, parents must establish and communicate to each child what these standards are, along with some warning of the penalty for disobedience. Penalties need to match children's psychological and physical capacities to comprehend and obey the rules at each age. In this process, personal accountability will be developed in each child.

As previously mentioned, the foundational biblical standards are obedience, the honor of parents, and respect for their right to rule. These are the foundations and mortar of the whole character-building process for children. These standards must be firmly established and maintained throughout the entire process of a child's growth and development. Additionally, parents must set their standards, for what they expect from their children through all three phases of their children's development. Within this framework, moral integrity and quality of character are formed in each child. This is accomplished by consistent rules that are clearly established and consistently enforced by parents.

Children also must be trained in attitude as well as in action. In every home, parents must teach self-control and manners, which includes the consideration of others. This is accomplished through specific "in-house" rules that every home develops for the pleasant functioning of an entire household. These rules must place value on mutual love and the development of each family member. In this environment, sacrificial love—one of the essential character qualities—will become present in the character of a child as he/she matures.

The goal of child training is to help children move as quickly as possible from external control to internal control or self-discipline. The purpose of discipline for our children is to lead them along a training pathway from dependence and immaturity to interdependence and personal accountability.

What happens when rules are broken in Phase Two? Rebuke and just punishment follow. Whereas chastisement is the appropriate discipline for willful disobedience or rebellion (attitude), rebuke and punishment are the God-given instruments for training our children toward personal accountability when standards or rules are broken (behavior). Rebuke and punishment are not appropriate until a rule or standard has been established and understood by our children. Children do not need to agree with every rule or standard, but they must understand them. Otherwise, discipline will not be fair. Moral integrity is established in this process.

Contrary to public opinion, there is an absolute standard of right and wrong for all behavior and conduct. There is a plumbline for all moral behavior. God's ten loving instructions explicitly establish these standards of behavior which become a strong moral compass for all of life.

When a child breaks a rule, a rebuke is the parent's declaration to the child that the specific action is wrong and unacceptable. The proper handling of this situation helps a child grow and teaches a child about the nature of God. A rebuke exposes sin, and guilt convicts the guilty person.

The real meaning of guilt has been obscured in our culture today. Guilt is not an emotional feeling. Guilt is the *fact* of having committed a known wrong. There are two *incorrect* ways to respond to the reality of having committed a known wrong: 1) justify the wrong with varying degrees of creativity, 2) blame our improper conduct on someone or something else. The *correct* way to deal with guilt is this: admit our known wrong and take personal responsibility for it. The correct alternative is called *confession*, which simply means to admit to a wrong.

In the context of training children, confession is the honest acknowledgment of having committed a wrong by a child to a parent. Honest admission is crucial to the development of character and necessary to eliminate the devastating effects of *hidden* guilt. Unconfessed guilt, when committing a known wrong, drives a wedge between parents and children. Confession is God's healing remedy to remove the alienation children feel with their parents because of having knowingly disobeyed. Confession of the known wrong by children, followed by the forgiveness[174] of parents, restores children's real and desperate need for acceptance. Forgiveness cleanses the guilt a child is experiencing and releases parents from the tension that conflict has produced. Forgiveness also prevents any buildup of animosity between parent and child.

It is the absence of love and acceptance that has devastating effects on the lives of children, not the presence of guilt. God designed sincere guilt to help lead to wholeness through the process of admitting wrong and receiving forgiveness. Ongoing intimacy of relationship and acceptance are part of the legacy of our hearts in which our children thrive and grow as they move toward

[174] Genuine forgiveness is composed of two elements. The first is a *pardon* from a wrong done and the second is the *forgetting* of a wrong done. Past wrongs are not to be brought up in the future and used against our children. In God's economy, life has the wonderful dimension of many new and fresh starts when failure has marred relationships. Rebuke, confession, and forgiveness, all our loving provisions of our heavenly Father are for our good. See Jer. 31:34, and Isa. 43:25.

personal accountability and maturity. Rebuke, followed by genuine confession and forgiveness, leads to the restoration of these primary relationships, which produces wholeness, enhances learning, and contributes to effective ongoing discipline to maturity.

Once our children have admitted to any wrong behavior which we expose by our rebuke, our forgiveness should be immediate and unconditional—just as God's forgiveness is to us when we fail in our relationship with Him, admit our wrongs, and receive His forgiveness. After a rebuke, our children need to feel reassured of our love and restored acceptance.

Whenever Gretchen and I disciplined our children, our goal was to make clear to our children that we were correcting wrong *behavior*. Never did we communicate to our children that we thought *they* were bad. Instead, we let them know that what they were *doing* was wrong.

On occasion, we disciplined our children twice for the wrong action. Once for improper *behavior* or breaking a rule and the second time for the display of a rebellious *attitude*. The defiant attitude may have shown itself along with the wrong behavior or later in response to our rebuke. At such times we would make clear to our children why they were being punished twice for one apparent misdeed. Rebellion (attitude) and wrong conduct (behavior) both must be disciplined and corrected.

Following such corrections, we would immediately lift our children into our arms to comfort them, communicate our acceptance, and explain the reasons for their correction. I shared the anguish our children were expressing as I held them close to me. These "after correction" times often become some of the most teachable moments during the early years. Parental authority is accepted more than any other time during these training sessions. Teaching the importance of standards, the meaning of obedience, guilt, confession, forgiveness, punishment, and restitution go straight to children's hearts during these moments. These experiences in the sandpile of life help to form our children's inner BIOS, which they will carry with them throughout life.

Andrew was well on his way into the young childhood phase, and discipline was seldom required. He seemed "older" to me, so I just began correcting and disciplining his occasional misdeeds without reassuring him of my love for him after disciplining him. After correcting him in this manner a few times, Andrew asked, "Daddy, why don't you pick me up anymore after you have disciplined me and hold me?" This incident helped me understand just how vital and important the second part[175] of this discipline process was (comfort, love, and acceptance) for reassuring our children of our love and closing the brief rift in our relationship. Though our children were corrected and disciplined, there was never any doubt in their minds that they were always loved through the whole process.

Confession (verbal agreement with a disclosed wrong) also enables children to face their parents with a clear conscience. It causes a child to realize personal responsibility for all his actions and attitudes. A child who has accepted his guilt will also receive punishment with a proper attitude. As a penalty for wrongdoing, discipline and restitution teach accountability. Following confession and forgiveness, punishment is administered without anger. Fair penalties for misbehavior are a fact of life that must be learned. Whereas the purpose of chastisement is to conquer rebellion and force proper submission to authority, punishment is the payment of just penalty for any type of wrong done. As God's established authority over children, a parent executes fair punishment when standards have been broken. Such discipline develops the proper

---

175 This was one very important concept I learned in reading James Dobson's Book, *Dare To Discipline*. This volume has been revised and is available by the title, *The New Dare To Discipline*.

fear of justice and respect for the power of authority. The administration of fair justice by a parent to a child proves the sureness of judgment and prepares a child to accept the rule of government and God.[176]

This is sorely needed in our world today as we all question whether justice truly exists. As a foundational element in authentic relational biblical learning, the administration of punishment by parents with their children can help reverse this false impression by instilling a respect for the consequences of broken standards. Every rule will have a reasonable discipline if the standard is broken. As parents, we determine appropriate punishments that are relevant to the ages of our children and fair with rules or standards that have been broken.

Punishment may also include fair restitution or the correct payment to right a wrong. God will give us insight into each disciplinary situation with our children if we ask Him. Parenting forces moms and dads to depend upon God daily for His wisdom!

When I was in grade school I threw a stick in my schoolyard, which unintentionally struck and seemed to crack a window. When I got home and told my mother what had happened, I was marched back to school and had to confess (admit to my guilt) for what I had done. My punishment (just compensation for the wrong) was to make payment for the window. I knew this before

[176] Romans 13 clearly outlines the origins of and attitude that we are to have toward government. Paul writes in Rom 13:1-5, "Obey the government, for God is the one who put it there. All governments have been placed in power by God. So those who refuse to obey the laws of the land are refusing to obey God, and punishment will follow. For the authorities do not frighten people who are doing right, but they frighten those who do wrong. So do what they say, and you will get along well. The authorities are sent by God to help you. But if you are doing something wrong, of course you should be afraid, for you will be punished. The authorities are established by God for that very purpose, to punish those who do wrong. So you must obey the government for two reasons: to keep from being punished and to keep a clear conscience."

I fearfully entered the room of the person who was in the office where my stick had struck the window. At that age, I was trying to fathom how I was ever going to come up with my portion of the GNP to pay for a replacement window. Much to my surprise, after my confession, the school official informed me the window was already cracked and that it had not been my doing. What a relief! Nevertheless, that experience still resides in my memory bank as an unforgettable lesson of the principle of making a payment or just compensation for committing a wrongdoing. (It also instilled in me a more comprehensive awareness of the need to look for more appropriate places for stick launching than next to the courtyard windows of school officials.)

There are times when it will be evident that our children who have become normally obedient and confess to a wrong, before even needing our rebuke, have already paid sufficient penalty without formal punishment. Such a response from our children— to acknowledge guilt *on their own*— comes because of consistently applied discipline and the development of our children's own internal guidance system and integrity. On occasion, while our children were growing up they would come to us with an unsolicited confession for a wrong about which we knew nothing. Upon hearing this honest acknowledgment for a wrong and seeing the agony of personal guilt already present in one of our children, we sometimes deemed that penalty enough for them. We would communicate our forgiveness and absorb the cost for payment that was due to them ourselves.

Under these circumstances, our actions taught our children another remarkable characteristic of Yahweh—His mercy.[177] Wrong actions always require someone to pay. In our love for our

[177] Mercy is the withholding of deserved punishment. God's mercy toward us is much deeper and richer than simply withholding just punishment. For those who receive Yeshua, God not only withholds death as our just punishment for our sin and rebellion toward God, but gives us eternal life. Such mercy

children, we paid the cost for a wrong which they had committed. How grateful they were and how much more our bonds of love with each other were strengthened through those experiences.

Discipline not only restrains the natural inclination toward corruption and teaches a standard of purity but reveals the nature of God to our children. In the process of disciplining our children, they learn that God's love includes discipline. Practically, children learn that God is just, merciful, and forgiving. Children learn that God cares about others as they are required to make restitution to those they have wronged. Children learn that guilt (the fact of committing a known wrong) is a positive force that helps bring them to confession (personal agreement with exposed wrongdoing), which leads to psychological and emotional wholeness. Children learn that God has provided rules for living that lead to joy, freedom, soundness, and maximum fulfillment. Children also learn that living within God's parameters rescues them from death, provides an entrance to life, and marks a sure course for the greatest adventure in living that can be experienced.

As soon as possible during Phase Two, verbal instruction must also include the *why* (reasons) behind the standards we are teaching our children. In the process of discipline, it is our children's understanding of the "why" of a rule or standard that helps them forge their concept of truth, reality, and accountability. Understanding the "why" of our word and biblical truth is the substance upon which our children ultimately build their authentic biblical basis for conduct and learning. Taking the time to answer the "why" questions during the second half of Phase Two discipline is essential for preparing our children to cross the threshold from childhood into young adulthood characterized by personal responsibility and accountability.

---

is incomprehensible but real. God Himself is its source. See Rom. 6:23 and John 3:16.

The goal of Phase One and Phase Two learning is summarized by Solomon in Proverbs 22:6. "Train a child in the way he should go, and when he is old, he will not turn from it." (NIV) Another rendering of this verse says. "Teach your children to choose the right path, and when they are older, they will remain upon it." (NLT) *Child* in this verse is the span of growth toward maturity on the age continuum from infant to age 12-13. This period in childhood is pliable compared to later years that become hard and unimpressible. Thus, in the environment of the home, parents initiate their children in the way of life from the earliest dawn of intelligence.[178]

As parents, we have the awesome responsibility of setting our children apart to the Lord as a temple newly built and not yet corrupt. By our early childhood training, we are dedicating our children as a temple of the Holy Spirit.

We are also to train our children in the "way they should go." The way they should go is the direction we want them to go because of our love for our children. This kind of love is expressed in our restraint, which will keep our children from going how they *would* go with their natural inborn bias toward corruption in attitude and behavior.

The phrase "he should go" comes from the Hebrew word *peh,* which means man's mouth. This reveals a deep and intriguing meaning to this phrase. The mouth is the external manifestation of one's character. It also is the organ through which one's relationship with God is ascertained. King David wrote, "Taste and see that the LORD is good. Oh, the joys of those who trust in him!"[179]

---

[178] Deut. 6:7; 2 Tim. 1:5; 3:15.

[179] Ps. 34:8. There is nothing more satisfying than the presence of God. It is better than the finest gourmet dining experience. David conveys this experience by writing, "O God, you are my God; I earnestly search for you. My soul thirsts for you; my whole body longs for you in this parched and weary land where there is no water. I have seen you in your sanctuary and

As we welcome and enjoy the presence of God in our own lives and obey Him with all our hearts, our children will taste (perceive), and feast on the Lord along with us. In so doing, they will experience for themselves that *He* is good. Helping our children to experience and savor the sweet presence of the Holy Spirit and the delight of keeping Yahweh's loving instructions[180] places an indelible flavor on their palate that will help train our children in the "way they should go" and to remain on it as they enter adulthood.

The pathway of discipline in God's design is to equip our children to exercise self-control based upon internalized standards, which is ultimately rooted in their relational fear of God.[181] As parents, we are to help guide our children into a lifestyle of moral conduct that is in harmony with standards they have embraced for themselves. These standards are deeply and personally rooted in genuine obedience to God and His loving instructions. Authentic biblical learning teaches that personal accountability is the hallmark of transition from childhood into young adulthood (about age 13). This is the beginning of Phase Three in the continuum of growth toward maturity.

---

gazed upon your power and glory. Your unfailing love is better to me than life itself; how I praise you! I will honor you as long as I live, lifting up my hands to you in prayer. You satisfy me more than the richest of foods. I will praise you with songs of joy. I lie awake thinking of you, meditating on you through the night. I think how much you have helped me; I sing for joy in the shadow of your protecting wings. I follow close behind you; your strong right hand holds me securely" Ps. 63:1-8, (NLT). Now, our lives and homes become the sanctuary of God's presence with us.

180 "God's laws are perfect. They protect us, make us wise, and give us joy and light. God's laws are pure, eternal, just. They are more desirable than gold. They are sweeter than honey dripping from a honeycomb. Ps 19:7-10. (TLB)

181 Please review Chapter 4, footnote 62 for the critical importance of coming to understand the fear of God. It is the cornerstone of biblical learning.

## *Phase Three*

Phase Three equipping/mentoring is the capstone that is built upon the sound and complete functioning of BIOS of love, bonding, and discipline.

In the absence of an authentic biblical view and understanding of personal accountability, our society calls this period "adolescence." In our culture, adolescence (age 12-20) has become a grim no-man's-land of free experimentation. This culture of death in the public arena leads youth searching for their identity into substance abuse, splintered and broken relationships, and even physical death.

Death stalks our youth as some become victims of violent murder by their peers or take their own lives through suicide. In the absence of an adult community that fears God and keeps His commandments, we are seeing the fruit of a generation that has been orphaned by their parents, searching for their identity in a fantasy world that encourages corruption without any awareness of immediate or future accountability. Adolescence has become an aberration in time in which the high value, significance, and potential of youth are systematically stolen, killed, and destroyed.[182]

The Hebraic concept of transition from childhood into the adult community is profoundly different than the one in which our youth are living today. This perspective has been practiced in Jewish communities for generations providing an immediate pathway to *life,* as well as many added years of productivity and contributions to others. As parents, we especially must grapple with this truth to understand what God's word teaches regarding young adulthood and then instruct our children with God's view

[182] This unguided search for fulfillment in the wrong direction produces the exact opposite of what is being sought. God desires the best for every person. In John 10:10 Jesus said, "The thief's purpose is to steal and kill and destroy. My purpose is to give life in all its fullness."

of reality and truth. His view is radically different than the culture's view in which we live.

Rather than abandoning adolescents to their subculture at a gateway to death through irresponsible and corrupt actions, early adult living in God's design places our teenagers at the gateway to life as responsible and accountable young men and women who have become a part of the adult community. This transitional moment in a person's experience of leaving childhood and becoming a part of the adult community is illustrated and celebrated in the Jewish ceremony of Bar Mitzvah (at age 13). Bar Mitzvah[183] is the formal acknowledgment and celebration that one's child is moving from childhood into adulthood.

In his book *To Life*, Harold Kushner writes, "In Jewish life, a child is under the authority of his or her parents until the age of thirteen. The assumption is that the child will obey the parents or that the parents will be able to control their child. Adolescents and grown children, however, are responsible for their behavior. The Bar/Bat Mitzvah ceremony celebrates the young person's coming of age, 'graduating' from childhood to adult status."[184] Kushner goes on to say that Bar Mitzvah has also been translated as "son of the commandment," which means "member of the mitzvah system," that is, a person both qualified and expected to perform the mitzvah in a way that he or she was too young to do before.

The idea behind Bar Mitzvah was understood by the second or third century. Age thirteen was seen as the legal age of responsibility. At this time, young Jews began to assume adult responsibilities. This was the time that a transition was made from being a child of whom little was demanded except obedience to becoming

183 Mitzvah is derived from the Hebrew word mitsvah which means: a) a commandment (of man), b) the commandment (of God), c) a commandment (of a code of wisdom).

184 Kushner, *To Life*, 221.

a responsible adult. Understanding and embracing personal responsibility was the goal of authentic biblical learning for children, and it initially occurred without any formal celebration. It was simply lived out as children were trained and entered responsible living in God's mitzvah (His commandments) and became directly accountable to God themselves. The actual ceremony of Bar Mitzvah was a late medieval invention[185] celebrating what had, for centuries, been the natural transition from childhood to responsible adult living.

For all of us, accountability has its roots in God. With utter simplicity, Solomon writes his conclusion for the meaning and purpose in life in Ecclesiastes 12:13, "Here is my conclusion: fear God and obey his commandments, for this is the entire duty of man." Not only does this lead to peace, fulfillment, and achievement in this life, but fearing God and keeping His commandments is of crucial importance for another reason. In verse 14, Solomon continues, "For God will judge us for everything we do, including every hidden thing, good or bad."[186] Whether men choose to acknowledge it or not, all of life leads to the final and ultimate accountability before God.

Our lives are short in comparison to eternity. At the end of each of our lives, God will bring every work into judgment, and every man's eternal state will be finally determined. God, Himself will be the Judge. He not only has the right to do so because He is God but as God/man, He is perfectly fit to do so. God is wise and just. On that final day, everything done in the body will be brought to remembrance and judged whether it was good or evil.

---

185 Ibid. 223-225.

186 Eccl. 12:14. (TLB)

Even secret things will be brought to light and to account on that judgment day.[187]

A straightforward criterion will be everyone's standard of judgment at that time. Is what we have done been conformable to the will of God or a violation of it? The certainty of this strict and ultimate accountability to God helps to motivate us to be careful in our walk with God. God has generously given us all the guidelines that we need so this final accounting before Him will be one that we can offer with joy.

It is our responsibility as parents to help our children to understand that their rite of passage from childhood into adulthood is a serious transition. We are transferring their accountability from us as parents directly to them. They now have their own responsibility before God. Equipping our children with this understanding will help give them the strength to withstand the destructive choices errantly made due to peer pressure while helping to preserve their well-being and guide them along the pathway to God's particular call for their lives.

Living within this personal awareness of direct accountability to God sets the stage for maximum benefit of the final equipping/mentoring in Phase Three of the growth continuum. Maximum Phase Three learning is the gift for those young adults who have embraced the fear of God and personal accountability before Him. Living within this accountability produces the most considerable freedom to learn and releases the highest skills in those called to mentor our children during this phase. This is the final phase

---

[187] "For it is not merely knowing the law that brings God's approval. Those who obey the law will be declared right in God's sight. Even when Gentiles, who do not have God's written law, instinctively follow what the law says, they show that in their hearts they know right from wrong. They demonstrate that God's law is written within them, for their own consciences either accuse them or tell them they are doing what is right. The day will surely come when God, by Jesus Christ, will judge everyone's secret life." (Rom. 2:13-16).

for providing all the elements that will bring the unique gifting, calling, and purpose into full blossom in the lives of our children.

Naturally, the mentoring/equipping process is one that will occur throughout all three phases of the growth continuum. It is our responsibility as parents to be on the lookout for the emergence of God's gifts, talents, and purpose for each of our children during the first two phases of their growth. In addition to supplying what is needed to help develop the particular skills and knowledge for our children to become equipped for their life's purpose, perhaps the most critical function we play for our children in this process is giving our encouragement and support to them.

Our encouragement is like nutrient-rich moisture in an orchard. Consistently applied, our words of encouragement, support, and approval will produce a bountiful harvest. In Romans 14:19, Paul writes, "So then let us pursue the things which make for peace and the building up of one another."[188] "Building up" comes from the Greek word, *oikodomeo*, which means to be a housebuilder. By our recognition and confirmation, we help to establish and construct the lives of our children to most fully express God's distinct design for their lives. During the first two phases, we work as architects to promote growth in godly wisdom, affection, grace, virtue, and holiness. During Phase Three, we confirm and encourage the full development of our children's uniquely emerging gifts, talents, and purposes in God's kingdom.

Phase Three equipping is a subject deserving of another whole volume of its own and is beyond the scope of this writing, which is devoted to the *foundations of wholehearted learning*.[189] It may be helpful at this point to combine the previous diagrams of the four

---

188 (NAS). See also 1 Th. 5:11.

189 For an excellent home curriculum consistent with wholehearted learning, see *The Heart of Wisdom Teaching Approach: Bible Based Homeschooling* by Robin Sampson.

relational foundations and the three learning phases to complete a visual picture for the process of authentic biblical learning.

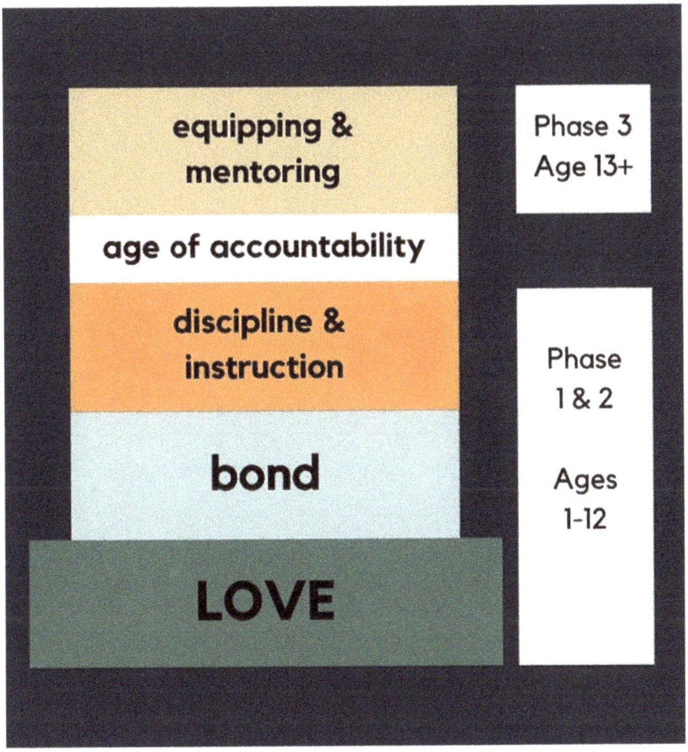


Equipping/mentoring is the diligent labor and sacrificial involvement that we as parents make in providing our children with the right environment, instruction, and skills to equip them for life. It is our God-given responsibility to provide all that our children need to reach healthy and productive maturity. Thankfully, we do not have to do everything ourselves. We can delegate. Phase Three is the time in which parents and the expanding community of teachers/mentors transfer the skills of competence to our children.

Secure in our love, and accountable before Yahweh, our children become young men and women who will be *effective* (do the right things) and *efficient* (doing things in the right way) with the help of our continuing encouragement. Effectiveness is built on instilled integrity of character. Efficiency is built upon the development of life, academic, and practical skills pertinent for each of our children to fulfill God's call on their lives.

There are no shortcuts to imparting the foundations of wholehearted biblical learning to our children. The rewards of faithful parenthood far surpass any occupational or economic achievement, position, or celebrity status. The greatest treasure on earth is God's *Shalom*. Happiness and peace of mind are God's intended gifts and lifetime treasures for parents who carefully and prayerfully keep His loving instructions themselves and raise their children in the discipline and instruction approved by the Lord. Our children will become achievers who live with well-guided purpose and integrity of character. Wholehearted learning cultivates *personal* wholeness, which results in a lifetime of meaningful accomplishments.

# Accepting the Challenge

*In* this book, I have endeavored to sketch a framework for establishing the foundations for wholehearted learning. I have attempted to write with fidelity to what is true and accurate according to God's word as I have understood it through His revelation and experience in our own lives over many years.

Our journey in knowing *Him* continues to this very moment. Knowing God is the greatest adventure in life. It is ongoing and continual. King David describes this adventure in Psalm 119:54-60 by saying, "Your principles have been the music of my life throughout the years of my pilgrimage. I reflect at night on who you are, O LORD, and I obey your law because of this. This is my happy way of life: obeying your commandments. LORD, you are mine! I promise to obey your words!With all my heart, I want your blessings. Be merciful, just as you promised. I pondered the direction of my life, and I turned to follow your statutes. I will hurry, without lingering, to obey your commands."

**Knowing God is the greatest adventure in life.**

Early in our marriage, God made very clear to me that the first two priorities He wanted me to live out in my life were: 1) to obey Him at any cost to myself, and 2) to sacrificially care for my wife and children. These are God's priorities. They were to be mine as well. In God's economy, occupational choices and church involvement/ministry are designed to *support* this primary mission, not usurp it. The pressure of conforming to the world around us and the sheer labor of daily living is constant and real threats to maintaining the kind of balance and focus we need to accomplish our goal as parents. We need the wisdom of God as parents for the choices we make so we might successfully fulfill God's mandate to us to "raise our children in the nurture and admonition of the Lord." He will help us discern the times and seasons for *what we do* and *how we spend our time* during the passages we all make through our lives.

Raising children is a season that is with us only once in our journey through this life. It cannot be recaptured. Beyond the direct influence we have on our children's lives, what we do during this season of our life impacts four generations!

God challenges us to test His word for ourselves to see if what He says is true.[190] As parents, Gretchen and I have thor-

[190] The Pharisees were continual skeptics and critics of Jesus during his earthly sojourn. In John 7:15 they questioned the source of Jesus' teaching. In

oughly tested His word regarding these foundations for biblical learning in the lives of our children. We have found every word given by God about His way of establishing these foundations completely trustworthy. The results have exceeded and continue to surpass anything we could have hoped. As parents, Gretchen and I have immense satisfaction as we observe the fruit, attitudes, and behavior in the lives of our three children.

Each one is walking in response to God's personal and ongoing direction for their own lives. They are leaders among their peers and excel in what they do. Most of all, they, too, are discovering how to make their obedience to God the priority in their own lives. All credit belongs to God. We are grateful for His love. We have simply been eyewitnesses to the grace of God at work in our lives and our home.

---

response, Jesus challenged them by saying, "If anyone chooses to do God's will, he will find out whether my teaching comes from God or whether I speak on my own." (vs. 17, NIV). Our scientific techno-culture often defiantly expresses the same notion, "Show me and I will do what you say." This is the hypothesis of scientific materialism. But God, who authored all science, challenges us by saying, "Do what I say and I will show you." God, who created the universe, also superintends and supersedes scientific discovery. He invites all *who will* to move beyond the confines of science into three-dimensional living. Faith is not a blind leap into some black hole, but a reasoned and intelligent response to God's trustworthy word and love for man which he repeatedly has demonstrated throughout history. As man responds to God's word in obedience, God shows (reveals to) man a new quality of life, meaning to existence, and wholeness in a living in *relationship* with the creator Himself. God's challenge to test the truth of His word is also an invitation to know how good He is. After describing God's *loving and merciful* involvement with man in all of history (see Romans chapters 1-11), Paul writes in Romans 12: 1-2, "...so, dear brothers and sisters, I plead with you to give your bodies to God. Let them be a living and holy sacrifice— the kind he will accept. When you think of what he has done for you, is this too much to ask? Don't copy the behavior and customs of this world, but let God transform you into a new person by changing the way you think. Then you will know what God wants you to do, and you will know how good and pleasing and perfect his will really is."

I asked Andrew, Elizabeth, and Jonathan to write a few thoughts and experiences that were significant to them in learning the fear of God as they were growing up in our home. I did not give them any guidelines about what to write, nor had they seen what I had been writing about foundations for wholehearted learning. As I reviewed what all three of our children had written, I was amazed at how well their life stories helped illustrate many of the principles that have been discussed.

Andrew, Elizabeth, and Jonathan's lives have become living examples of the effectiveness of applying the foundations for authentic biblical learning in our home. We hope and pray their stories of growing up together in our family will encourage you to persevere as parents as you seek to establish the foundations for wholehearted, authentic biblical learning. God desires the absolute best for you and your precious children. His loving instructions are priceless. His love is unfailing.

## *Andrew*

I was always an adventurous kid. I still am— yes, both adventurous and a kid (well, an excessively big one)—even though I have children of my own now. And I have come to understand many things to which I was oblivious when I was younger. Here is one example. It is the tale of one of my adventures that taught me an unbelievably valuable lesson. It marked just one of my transitions from modes of childlike thought to gaining a more mature awareness of cause and effect, action, and consequence. I use similar true stories with my children when I am trying to help them gain some wisdom that can often only sink in in a hard way.

I grew up in the country almost 10 miles outside Russellville, a small town in Arkansas. It was a wonderful place for an adventurous boy. Plenty of woods to explore, lots of lands to conquer, that sort of thing. About a mile or so through the woods behind my best friend's house were some bluffs, which had provided fantastic exploration on many occasions. Another mile or two past those bluffs, we discovered a mysterious ghost town. I say "ghost town," but it was only a few houses, a couple of barns, and maybe one or two shops that had been falling apart and yielding the space back to nature for many years before we even found them. But there they were, in the middle of the woods. The vague impression of an overgrown road or two could almost be distinguished, but the tall grass and trees obscured them as just another part of the forest to casual observation. You can probably imagine the intrigue and curiosity surrounding this place for a ten-year-old boy. Especially a boy who found a town where one wasn't expected or supposed to be.

We learned the legend later from my friend's dad. It was a place once called Shinsville. Two families had initially settled in the area: the Russells and the Shins. There was some heated controversy as to whether the area should be named Shinsville or Russellville. I guess the Shins lost. But it was exciting to investigate what they had left behind for us to discover.

One day, my best friend and a couple of our buddies came over, asking if I wanted to go exploring with them. I knew that meant hiking out to Shinsville. It was not a frequent excursion, and I desperately wanted to be part of the expedition. The only catch: I was supposed to take a nap that afternoon.

After much pleading (and probably a good deal of my renowned lawyer-level logic, which for some reason my parents called "arguing"), my mother gave her reluctant permission for me to go. I was ecstatic. During the whole adventure, I could not help but smugly bask in my confidence that my persistence had been worth it.

It was quite a trek there and back, so I did not get home until well into the evening, and I was exhausted. I was so tired I was even willing to go to bed early to hopefully smooth things over with Mom and make up for that nap that I had missed. However, not long after I got back, the phone rang.

Do you know that one-of-a-kind childhood friend, the truly amazingly good kind? The kind who lived a long drive away across town, so it was almost impossible ever to go over and play? The kind who had all the newest and best toys and the most video games out of all your other friends combined? Well, yeah, the lady on the phone talking to my mom at that moment was the mother of that kind of friend. And he was inviting me to spend the night that very night (of all nights), which was by far rarer and more special than an expedition to Shinsville.

I found myself begging Mom again, because—as you've probably put together— although I never had that nap, I NEEDED to be up all night playing Nintendo. If only I had just taken that nap in the first place, sacrificing what I wanted in the short term, I would have received a mind-blowing, unexpected guilt-free reward in return.

Why she let me go in the end, I'll never know for sure. I asked her about it later in life, and she did not remember the story at all. But the memory was indelibly imprinted on my mind because I felt terrible. I was getting everything I wanted that day, but as Mom drove me to my friend's house in the dark, I was gaining a sense of the cost of my shortsightedness and realizing there was a wise and bigger perspective hidden behind the things my parents ask me to do. I had often done everything in my power to avoid those very things without understanding the wisdom I was avoiding at the same time.

Some might say such practical lessons, which hopefully come to most of us by adulthood, make life more complicated. When we think about obeying commandments and following rules, our first natural reaction can easily be "What a hassle! Look at all this stuff

I must worry about doing. I'd rather just be free to do what I want." I submit that the perspective gained through this story from my childhood helps simplify everything greatly. Once we understand there are more significant reasons for God's commandments—wisdom more in-depth than we can immediately see—the arguing and begging and justifying other courses of action no longer seem so smart. We can still choose our path and individual steps along the way, of course. But it feels far superior to make those choices based on the instructions of our Creator who already knows all effects before their causes even happen. If we apply that to every area of our lives, we will always know what to do. God is trying to shield us from the complex consequences, which are set in motion when we avoid simple, trusting obedience.

## *Elizabeth*

I am who I am today because of who my parents are. Growing up in Russellville, Arkansas, amidst the unpaved roads and wild blackberry patches, I was not aware of a grander world. My world was my parents, two brothers, and the one-and-a-half acres upon which we lived. I learned the fundamental lessons of life in this setting, through the discipline and love of my parents.

Discipline and love. Those are the tools my parents used to raise me. I learned what it means to fear the Lord through the holy fear I had of my mother if I disobeyed her. Spanking was never a dilemma in our house. If I was disobedient, I was punished. But it was always made clear to me why I was being punished, and when the dreaded paddling was finished, it was always made clear to me that it was done out of love. Of course, at four years old, one questions the veracity of that, but I always knew it was because my parents loved me so much that they would discipline me. I could tell they took no pleasure in punishing me. And I certainly took no pleasure in being punished. Therefore, I strove to obey my parents. My actions had consequences. This healthy respect for authority has served me throughout my life as I've navigated school, jobs, and becoming a parent myself.

However, love has certainly encompassed a more significant part of my life than discipline. I could not even attempt to list all the things my parents have done for me and my brothers, all the sacrifices they have made out of genuine love. My mom became a schoolteacher, surrendering her time at home, to provide a way for Andrew, Jonathan, and me to attend a private Christian school. Not only did this get us out of the mediocre public-school system in Virginia Beach, but it gave us a school in which we could be challenged academically and spiritually, and develop deep friendships that we may not have found elsewhere. My mom had always been a homemaker, but to give us this opportunity we needed the extra paycheck. She willingly taught for 15 years.

I remember one specific instance, from which I gleaned the measure of my dad's love for me. It was quite practical and straightforward, but I still remember it so clearly. When I was in eighth grade, I had a difficult pre-algebra teacher. We were required to do a math lesson every night for homework and the next day we would check our answers in class. These lessons counted as quiz grades, so I realized I needed some help when I would get 10 out of 30 wrong. I brought this problem to my dad. Instead of getting upset at me, as some fathers, unfortunately, might do, he offered to help. Every night he would personally check every sum, every equation, and when he found one I had worked wrong, he would help me through it until I discovered the right answer. He was so patient. I went from getting ten wrong to only missing one or two, and often, none. By being so involved in such a simple thing as my schoolwork, my dad showed his love for me.

Now that I am a mother myself of two beautiful children, I am so grateful for the foundation that my parents laid for me. Parenting is scary— nothing can prepare you for what it takes. But thankfully, I have had tools and resources for how to deal with my kids when they need discipline. And of course, showing them the kind of unconditional, sacrificial love my parents taught me and my brothers has been and always will be my goal.

A text from my 14-year-old daughter when she was at a sleepover recently: "Goodnight mommy!! I love you to the moon and back! I'm so blessed and thankful to have you as my mom! You are such a beautiful person inside and out, and you are just so so amazing! Thank you so much for absolutely everything and for all you do! You are the best mom ever! I cannot wait to see you in the morning! I pray that you have a really good sleep and sweet dreams! Love you!"

When you admonish and treasure your children, they know it. And it becomes the well they draw from for the rest of their lives.

## *Jonathan*

My dad and mom have deposited a lot of good things into my life, from general love and time they poured into me to lessons they taught me, either directly or by example. As an adult now and parent myself looking back over my years growing up, I think of a few highlights of my upbringing that were incredibly impactful for me.

### Always Keep Pursuing God and Learning

I have observed that my parents have a willingness and desire always to keep learning. This trait translated into the same for our family. I think of this particularly in the arena of faith and spiritual walk, by seeking to know God more intimately, understanding and living out His word, and participating with Him as He unfolds the fulfillment of biblical prophecy in our lifetime.

While my parents and our family would look at other topics too, the primary aspect I remember was focus on God and His ways. It was not about being merely knowledgeable or well-studied but rather a pursuit of God Himself.

Over the years I have continually seen my parents reading books and newsletters, listening to tapes/CDs/radio programs, etc. (yes, I grew up in the '80s and '90s). These activities were very much a shared family journey that included my siblings and me as we grew up, not something my parents would only do on their own. They shared tidbits from their current reading or listening material, and regularly we would be doing these activities all together as a family. We gleaned from resources from different ministries and teachers across a decently broad spectrum, actively participated in local churches/congregations/home groups (including learning, discussing Scripture, and praying with adults and children together), went to conferences, and so on.

My parents' example, and the shared family journey, has taught me the humility to recognize none of us has "arrived" yet in a full understanding of God or even other areas of life, which I believe is very important to keep us teachable. Being teachable is extremely helpful to have the capacity to learn and sometimes even unlearn and relearn how we previously understood things.

Secondly, my parents' ongoing learning demonstrates a yearning, a motivation to love and walk with God to the fullest and not settle just for what we already know or have experienced, as true (though incomplete) as it may be.

Perhaps this example of humility and eagerness to continually press on in pursuit of God will inspire readers of this book in their role as parents or even in chewing on its contents for themselves.

## Life is a Learning Opportunity

I remember several situations where my dad would use a life situation to teach me a principle about parenting or life. For example, I remember being in public settings observing another family with a child, and he would discuss some of the dynamics of what was happening and how to help the child. The goal was to equip me with practical wisdom about how to understand and handle different situations, not to assess or critique another family's parenting. Overall, life tips gleaned from real-life situations have accumulated over time and given me tools in my tool belt to use now as a parent. Children are not just children but also future parents, God willing.

## Discipline out of Love

When my parents disciplined me growing up, they would say, "I'm doing this because I love you." I did not understand this as a child, at least in full, since receiving a spanking (e.g., for disobedience or doing wrong) was an unpleasant experience (albeit temporary). Even though I did not understand it at the time, I am so glad they communicated their love to me, not merely giving physical discipline, and that they did discipline me because of their love for me. Regardless of the method of discipline used, I think doing it from a motivation of love for the benefit of our children is what our heavenly Father would desire for us as we seek to model Him.

As a parent with two young children, I am starting to see firsthand how raising and training children is an involved process. While training them to listen and obey, there can be many moments where we are tempted to respond out of disappointment, frustration, or anger. To be honest, I do sometimes fall short, succumbing to those feelings in the heat of the moment (which are great opportunities to show humility and ask forgiveness from our children, too). However, I believe I have a framework for understanding how training and discipline (there are many aspects of these beyond just correction for times of noncompliance) can be done out of love in the genuine best interest of my children, based on what my parents instilled in me and, with Yahweh's help, will continue to grow in my heart.

I hope that sharing some of the character, examples, and actions of my parents that have impacted and benefited me over the years as a follower of Messiah and now as a parent will inspire other fellow parents as we together continue the journey of pursuing God and raising our children.

# Saplings of the LORD

*Playing* in the sandpile of life with our children is no easy task. Tending a garden takes time, but the rewards of reaping a bountiful harvest are immense. Nourishing our children in the love and discipline of the LORD is a long-term process that yields unspeakable rewards.

In the wisdom of God, He first invites us to become watchful caretakers of our hearts. The cultivation of His life in us waters and nourishes the tender lives of our children. For a season, our children are given to us so that we can instruct them to learn the fear of Yahweh and to take great delight in His law.

The foundational goals of biblical learning are both simple and profound. Since we all are to become true offspring of our heavenly Father, we first are to become like Him in righteousness, wisdom, and humility.

Our children become recipients of the legacy of our hearts. Together we are to become the saplings of the LORD.

My prayerful desire for you, the reader, is that in the reading of these words, you have discovered some of God's treasures for your own life and your precious children. I can think of no more appropriate manner to conclude this writing than to offer you the gift of God's word written for us by King David and Solomon, his son. I pray that God gives you grace and tenacity to tend the garden of your heart and children well.

Psalms 1 and Psalms 127-128 brush artistic word pictures of this process. Verse 6 in Psalm 1 states, "The LORD watches over the path of the godly." Godly means *righteous* in Hebrew. It conveys an all-encompassing meaning that is profoundly beautiful and desperately needed in the moral and ethical morass of our culture. Saplings of the LORD are righteous (as justified and vindicated by God) because of their simple trust in the redemption of God for their lives through the blood of Jesus Christ. They are just and righteous *in government.* They are just and right *in their cause.* They are just and upright *in conduct and character.*

The fear of the LORD is clean and endures forever. It is the beginning of wisdom and the pathway to life.

## *Words from King David and his son Solomon*

Psalm 1:1-6

"Oh, the joys of those who do not follow the advice of the wicked, or stand around with sinners, or join in with scoffers. But they delight in doing everything the LORD wants; day and night, they think about his law. They are like trees planted along the riverbank, bearing fruit each season without fail. Their leaves never wither, and in all they do, they prosper. But this is not true of the wicked. They are like worthless chaff, scattered by the wind. They will be condemned at the time of judgment. Sinners will have no place among the godly. For the LORD watches over the path of the godly, but the path of the wicked leads to destruction."

Psalm 127-128

"It is useless for you to work so hard from early morning until late at night, anxiously working for food to eat; for God gives rest to his loved ones. Children are a gift from the LORD; they are a reward from him. Children born to a young man are like sharp arrows in a warrior's hands. How happy is the man whose quiver is full of them! He will not be put to shame when he confronts his accusers at the city gates. How happy are those who fear the LORD—all who follow his ways! You will enjoy the fruit of your labor. How happy you will be! How rich your life! Your wife will be like a fruitful vine, flourishing within your home. And look at all those children! There they sit around your table as vigorous and healthy as young olive trees. That is the LORD's reward for those who fear him. May the LORD continually bless you from Zion. May you see Jerusalem prosper as long as you live. May you live to enjoy your grandchildren. And may Israel have quietness and peace."

***Shalom!***

# Bibliography


Ambre, K. Denise, 2020, https://www.ambreassociates.com/about-us.

Rebecca Chicot and Robert Winston, "The importance of early bonding on the long-term mental health and resilience of children. London Journal of Primary Care," Retrieved on Feb. 24, 2016, https://www.ncbi.nlm.nih.gov/pmc/articles/PMC5330336/#idm139960142451152title.

Campbell, Ross Dr., *How to Really Love Your Child.* Wheaton, IL: Victor Books, 1977.

Campbell, Ross Dr. *How to Really Love Your Teenager.* Wheaton, IL: Victor Books, 1981.

Dobson, James. *Dare to Discipline.* Wheaton, IL: Tyndale House, 1970.

Dobson, James. *The New Dare to Discipline.* Wheaton, IL: Tyndale House, 1992.

Dodson, Dr. Fitzhugh. *How to Father.* United States: New American Library, 1975.

Dodson, Dr. Fitzhugh. *How to Parent.* United States: Signet books, 1970.

Fugate, J. Richard. *What the Bible Says About Child Training.* Tempe, AZ: Aletheia Publishers, 1980.

Gilbertson, James. *PC Study Bible for Windows.* November 1998. http://www.Biblesoft.com.

Hanuck, Stephanie. "What Schools Are Getting Wrong on Discipline." Retrieved January 6, 2020, https://www.weareteachers.com/school-discipline-failures.

Harris, R. Laird, Gleason L. Archer, Jr., K. Waltke Bruce, *Theological Wordbook of the Old Testament.* Chicago: Moody Bible Institute, 1980.

"Harvard: 400 Years of Faith: *The Forerunner International* Vol. 1, No. 1. Fall, 1997.

Herbermann, Charles George, *The Catholic Encyclopedia, Vol. 4*, New York: Robert Appleton Company, 1912.

Heschel, Abraham J. *Insecurity of Freedom.* New York: Schocken Books, 1972.

Heschel, Abraham J. *The Prophets.* New York: Harper & Row, 1962.

Huges, R. Kent. *Disciplines of Grace.* Wheaton:Crossway Books, 1993.

Joy, Dr. Donald M. *Bonding*. Nappanee, IN:Evangel, 1987.

Kalman, Matthew. *USA Today*. Feb. 17, 1999.

Kushner, Harold S., *To Life!: A Celebration of Jewish Being and Thinking*. New York: Warner Books, 1993.

May, Rollo, *Love and Will.* New Yor.: W.W. Norton & Co, 1969.

NRLC. National Right to Life Releases 7th Annual Report on "State of Abortion in the United States," January 22, 2020. https://www.nrlc.org/communications/releases/2020/0122saus.

O'Hanlon, Ann. "Time Out for Alan." *The Washington Post Magazine.* June 21, 1998.

Palmer, Parker. *To Know as We Are Known, A Spirituality of Education.* San Francisco: Harper & Row, 1983.

Patterson, John. *The Wisdom of Israel.* Nashville: Abingdon Press, 1961.

Simmons, Dave. *Dad the Family Coach.* Wheaton, IL: Victor Books, 1992.

Simmons, Dave. *Dad the Family Counselor.* Wheaton, IL: Victor Books, 1992.

Simmons, Dave. *Dad the Family Mentor.* Wheaton, IL: Victor Books, 1992.

Snaith, Norman H. *The Distinctive Ideas of the Old Testament.* New York: Schocken Books, 1964.

Stern, David. *Jewish New Testament Commentary.* Maryland: Jewish New Testament Publications, 1992.

Strong, James. *Strong's Exhaustive Concordance of the Bible.* Abingdon Press, 1890.

Webster, Noah. *1828 American Dictionary of the English Language.* Foundation for American Christian Education; Facsimile of 1st edition, 1967.

White, Burton L., Ph.D. *Educating the Infant and Toddler.* Lexington, MA: D.C. Heath & Co, 1988.

Wilson, Marvin R., *Our Father Abraham.* Grand Rapids. MI: Wm. Eerdmans, 1989.

Zimmerman, Martha. *Celebrate the Feasts.* Minneapolis. MN: Bethany Fellowship. 1981.

# Further Reading


Alex, Marlee. *The Intimate Family, Hope for Hurried Homes*. Sisters. OR: Questar, 1990.

Allison, K. J. *Teaching Children as the Spirit Leads*. Plainfield, NJ: Logos, 1977.

Anderson, Neil T. and Steve Russo, *The Seduction of Our Children*. Eugene, OR: Harvest House,1991.

Babbitt, Kathy. *Habits of the Heart*. Brentwood, TN: Wolgemuth & Hyatt, 1990.

Berkowitz, Ariel & D'vorah. *Torah Rediscovered*. Littleton, CO: First Fruits of Zion, 1996.

Blumenfeld, Samuel L. *Is Public Education Necessary*? Boise, D: Paradigm, 1981.

Christenson, Larry. *Christian Families*. Minneapolis: Bethany Fellowship, 1970.

Covey, Stephen R. *The 7 Habits of Highly Effective People*. NY: Fireside, 1989.

Dargatz, Jan. *52 Simple Ways to Tell Your Child, "I Love You."* Nashville, TN: Olivet-Nelson Books, 1991.

Dobson, Dr. James, and Gary L Bauer. *Children at Risk, The Battle for the Hearts and Minds of Our Kids*. Dallas, TX: Word, 1990.

Dobson, Dr. James. *Parenting Isn't for Cowards*. Dallas, TX: Word, 1987.

Dobson. Dr. James. *Preparing for Adolescence, Straight Talk to Teens and Parents*. Ventura, CA: Regal Books, 1978.

Donaldson, Margaret, *Children's Minds*. NY: W. W. Norton, 1978.

Duckworth, Eleanor, *"The Having of Wonderful Ideas," and Other Essays on Teaching and Learning*. NY: Teachers College Press, 1987.

Durfield, Richard CL, Ph.D. and Renee Durfield. *Raising Them Chaste, A Practical Strategy for Helping Your Teen Wait till Marriage*. Minneapolis: Bethany House, 1991.

Elkind, David. *Child Development and Education, A Piagetian Perspective*. NY: Oxford University Press, 1976.

Exley, Richard. *The Rhythm of Life, Putting Life's Priorities in Perspective*. Tulsa, OK: Honor Books, 1987.

Hammond, Frank and Ida Mae, *Kingdom Living for the Family*, Kirkwood, MO: Impact Books, 1985.

Harris, Greg. *The Christian Home School*. Brentwood, TN: Wolgemuth & Hyatt, 1988.

Hayford, Jack. *Glory on Your House*. Tarrytown, NY: Fleming H. Revell Co., 1991.

Horne, Herman Harrell, *Teaching Techniques of Jesus*. Grand Rapids, MI: Kregel, 1987.

Garborg, Rolf. *The Family Blessing*. Dallas, TX:Word, 1990.

Getz, Gene A. *The Measure of a Family*. Ventura, CA: Regal Books, 1976.

Greenspan, Stanley M.D. *The Essential Partnership, How Parents and Children Can Meet the Emotional Challenges of Infancy and Childhood*. NY: Viking Penguin, 1989.

Klein, Isaac, *A Guide to Jewish Religious Practice*. NY: The Jewish Theological Seminary of America, Dist. by Ktav Publishing House, 1992.

Leman, Dr. Kevin. *Keeping Your Family Together When The World is Falling Apart*. NY: Delacorte Press, 1992.

Lucas, J.R. *The Parenting of Champions*. Brentwood, TN: Wolgemuth & Hyatt, 1989.

Lewittes, Mendel. *Jewish Marriage*. Northvale, NJ:Jason Aronson, 1994.

McClung, Floyd Jr. *The Father Heart of God*. Eugene, OR: Harvest House, 1985.

Meeks, Steve. *Relational Christianity*. Houston, TX: Calvary Publications, 1991.

Moore, Raymond S. and Dorothy N. *Better Late Than Early*. Washougal, WA: Reader's Digest Press, 1975.

Moore, Raymond S. and Dorothy N. *School Can Wait*. UT: Brigham Young University Press, 1979.

Phillips, Benny & Sheree. *Raising Kids Who Hunger For God*. Tarrytown, NY: Fleming H. Revell Co., 1991.

Sandford, John and Paula. *Restoring the Christian Family*. Plainfield, NJ: Logos International, 1979.

Sherrer, Quin with Ruthanne Garlock. *How to Pray for Your Family and Friends, Releasing God's Power in the. Lives of Your Spouse, Parents, Brothers, Sisters, Neighbors, and Even Your Enemies*. Ann Arbor, MI: Servant Publications, 1990.

Simmons, Dave. *Fatherhood Institute*. Wheaton, IL: Victor Books, 1992.

Smalley, Gary & John Trent, Ph.D. *The Blessing*. New York: Pocket Books, 1986.

Veith, Gene Edward, Jr. *Loving God with All Your Mind.* Westchester, L: Crossway Books, 1987.

Whitehead, John W. *The Rights of Religious Persons in Public Education.* Wheaton, IL: Crossway, 1991.

As our modern culture progressively opposes traditional and Godly values, it can become increasingly difficult for parents to feel confident in their methods for raising their children with wholeness and character. Thankfully, God's Word provides definitive instruction.

Pressing into the Bible, the research of experts, and his own parenting experiences, author Ron Lundquist helps parents rediscover God's loving instructions for a solid foundation at home and shows parents how to raise children so they can mature into responsible, well-educated, fulfilled adults.

Touching on the importance of healthy dynamics between married parents, the role and practice of discipline, testimonials from the author's children, and more, this book approaches each topic through a God-centered lens to direct parents the way He intended.

Whether you find yourself at a loss as a brand-new parent or are seeking guidance along the way, this book is for you.

---

With joint master's degrees in education and Biblical studies, Ron Lundquist accepted the invitation to be an adjunct professor and co-developed Regent University's first graduate course on character development for Christian educators. Ron and his wife, Gretchen, have raised three wholehearted children and now live in Colorado, where Ron is a published photographer, enjoys sports, and is an avid outdoorsman.

**"PUT THE PSYCHOLOGY BOOKS & SOCIAL PROPAGANDA MANUALS BACK ON THE SHELF, FOLKS – 'WHOLEHEARTED LEARNING' IS A CHILD-REARING BOOK FOR REAL PARENTS RAISING REAL CHILDREN IN A REAL WORLD."**

Bill Bullock, AAL, Bullock Law Firm

CPSIA information can be obtained
at www.ICGtesting.com
Printed in the USA
BVHW061526060421
604345BV00007B/795

9 781662 812286